EARLIER POEMS

OF

ELIZABETH BARRETT BROWNING

THE EARLIER POEMS OF ELIZABETH BARRETT BROWNING

1826-1833

LONDON
Bartholomew Robson Cranbourn-street
M.DCCC.LXXVIII.

INTRODUCTION.

Elizabeth Barrett Barrett, afterwards Elizabeth Barrett Browning, the foremost of English poetesses, and with the single exception of Sappho, of whom only some noble fragments remain to us, the foremost poetess of all time, was born in the year 1809, and was consequently in her seventeenth year when her earliest Poems were published—"verse," as an accomplished critic has lately remarked, "upon which was the stamp of true genius—poems eminently worthy of preservation."*

"It appears," says the writer of an article in the *Edinburgh Review*, "that her father encouraged her love for rhyme, since she has not only inscribed her collected poems to him in a dedication, written with great delicacy and tenderness of feeling, but in her

* Mr. G. Barnett Smith in an article on "Elizabeth Barrett Browning," in the new (ninth) edition of the *Encyclopædia Britannica*, vol. iv. (1877), p. 391.

earliest published volume there is also a poem addressed to him containing the lines :—

'For 'neath thy gentleness of praise,
My Father! rose my early lays!
And when the lyre was scarce awake,
I loved its strings for *thy* loved sake:
Woo'd the kind Muses—but the while
Thought only how to win thy smile.'

The small volume from which the above lines are taken, was published anonymously in 1826, and entitled 'An Essay on Mind, and other Poems,' with the modest motto from Tasso, '*Brama assai, poco spera, e nulla chiede*,' and is remarkable principally for the ambition of the young authoress; who after citing the authority of 'that immortal writer we have just lost,' (Byron), to prove that 'ethical poetry is the highest of all poetry, as the highest of all objects is moral truth,' proceeds at once to grapple with an ethical subject as wide as the universe itself. The poem is written in heroic verse, and extends over eighty-eight pages. The quality of the verse is not much above the level of Hayley or Miss Seward; but is remarkable for the precocious audacity with which she deals with the greatest names in the whole range of literature and science. Gibbon, Berkeley, Condillac, Plato,

Bacon, Bolingbroke, all come in for treatment in the scope of the young girl's argument. The minor poems, however, which conclude the volume, show much greater promise of originality."*

A lapse of seven years occurred before the publication of Elizabeth Barrett's next volume, which appeared in 1833, in her twenty-fourth year. The translation of the *Prometheus Bound* of Æschylus, which opened it, was replaced by the authoress in later years by an entirely new version. We have therefore not thought it wise or desirable to re-produce the earlier crude attempt or the girlish preface that accompanied it. But the original poems which followed —far in advance, as might be expected, of those in her first volume—are, for the most part, in no sense immature, or unworthy of the genius of the writer,—notably the *Vision of Life and Death*, the lines entitled, *Earth*, 'comparatively free from the stiffness of most of her blank verse, and surely a powerful composition;'† the lines *To a Poet's Child*, full of terrible

* *Edinburgh Review*, Oct. 1861, p. 515.

† *Quarterly Review*, Sept. 1840, § MODERN ENGLISH POETESSES—*Miss Barrett.*

irony and suppressed bitterness, *The Image of God*, *The Appeal*, *Idols*, *Weariness*, and several others.

The "exquisite touch" that "bides in the birth of things" is peculiarly apparent in the first bursting into bud and leaf of a new poetic genius. The summer of its manifestation may have greater fervour, and richer pomp and majesty of foliage, but about its early spring there must always be a nameless and peculiar charm. And therefore all that is best and worthiest in this book is to such a poem as *Aurora Leigh*, as an exquisite day of April is to a fervid day in August. Both have their own glory and sweetness; but the perfect summer flowers, be it remembered, were always reared "from seeds of April's sowing."

The cycle of Elizabeth Barrett's earlier work is completed by her third volume, entitled *The Seraphim and other Poems*, published in 1838, in her twenty-ninth year. Some of the minor poems in this book had appeared during the two previous years in the *Athenæum* and the *New Monthly Magazine*. Such of these pieces as have not been included in her Collected Writings may be added to a future edition of the present volume, should it prove acceptable to poetical students.

AN
ESSAY ON MIND,
WITH
OTHER POEMS.

"BRAMA ASSAI, POCO SPERA, E NULLA CHIEDE."
Tasso.

LONDON:
JAMES DUNCAN, PATERNOSTER-ROW.
MDCCCXXVI.

PREFACE.

IN offering this little Volume to the world, it is not my intention to trespass long on its indulgence, "with prefaces, and passages, and excusations." As, however, preface-writing strangely reminds one of Bottom's prologuizing device, which so ingeniously sheweth the 'disfiguration of moonshine,' and how lion was no lion after all, but plain "Snug the joiner," I will treat the subject according to my great prototype; declaring to those readers who "cannot abide lions," that their "parlous fear" is here unnecessary, and assuring the public that 'moonshine' shall be introduced as seldom as is consistent with modern composition.

But something more is necessary; and since writers commonly make use of their prefaces as opportunities for auricular confession to the absolving reader, I am prepared to acknowledge, with unfeigned humility, that the imputation of presumption is likely to be attached to me, on account of the form and title of this production. And yet, to imagine that a confidence in our powers is undeviatingly shewn by our selection of an extensive field for their exertion, is an error; for the subject supports the writer, as much as it is supported by him. It is not difficult to draw a succession of affecting images from objects intrinsically affecting; and ideas arising from an elevated subject are naturally elevated. As Tacitus hath it, "materiâ aluntur." Thought catches the light reflected from the object of her contemplation, and, "expanded by the genius of the spot," loses much of her material grossness; unless indeed, like Thales, she fall into the water while looking at the stars.

"Ethical poetry," says that immortal writer we have lost, "is the highest of all poetry, as the highest of all earthly objects must be moral truth." I am nevertheless aware how often it has been asserted that poetry is not a proper vehicle for abstract ideas—how far the assertion may be correct, is with me a matter of doubt. We do not deem the imaginative incompatible with the philosophic, for the name of Bacon is on our lips; then why should we expel the argumentative from the limits of the poetic? If indeed we consider Poetry as Plato considered her, when he banished her from his republic; or as Newton, when he termed her "a kind of ingenious nonsense;" or as Locke, when he pronounced that "gaming and poetry went usually together;" or as Boileau, when he boasted of being acquainted with two arts equally useful to mankind—"writing verses, and playing at skittles,"—we shall find no difficulty in assenting to this opinion. But while we behold in poetry, the inspiritings to political feeling, the "monumentum ære perennius" of buried nations, we are loth to believe her unequal to the higher walks of intellect: when we behold the works of the great though erring Lucretius, the sublime Dante, the reasoning Pope—when we hear Quintillian acknowledge the submission due from Philosophers to Poets, and Gibbon declare Homer to be "the law-giver, the theologian, the historian, and the philosopher of the ancients," we are *unable* to believe it. Poetry is the enthusiasm of the understanding; and, as Milton finely expresses it, there is "a high reason in her fancies."

As, according to the plan of my work, I have dwelt less on the operations of the mind than on their effects, so I have not touched on that point difficult to argue, and impossible to determine—the nature of her substance. The investigation is curious, and the subject a glorious one; but, after all, our closest reasonings thereupon are acquired from analogy, and our most extensive views must be content to take their places among other ingenious speculations. The columns of Hercules are yet unpassed. Metaphysicians have cavilled and confuted; but they have failed in their endeavour to establish any permanent theoretical edifice on that windy site. The effort was vainly made even by our enlightened Locke; and, as in the days of Socratic disputation, it is still given to the learned to ask, though not to answer, 'τί δὲ ἡ ψυχὴ.' Perhaps, however, the following sensible acknowledgment would better become their human lips, than the most artfully constructed hypothesis—The things we understand are so excellent, that we believe what we do not understand to be likewise excellent.*

The effects of mental operation, or productions of the mind, I have divided into two classes—the philosophical, and the poetical; the former of which I have subdivided into three divisions—History, Physics, and Metaphysics: History, or the doctrine

* I here adopt, with some little variation, an expression which fell from Socrates, on the subject of a work by Heraclitus the obscure.

of man, as an active and social being; Physics, or the doctrine of efficient causes; Metaphysics, or the doctrine of abstractions, and final causes. Lord Bacon's comprehensive discernment of the whole, and Locke's acute penetration into parts, have assisted me in my trembling endeavour to trace the outline of these branches of knowledge. To have considered them methodically, and in detail, would have greatly exceeded both the limits of my volume, and, what is more material, the extent of my information: but if I may be allowed to hope that

"The lines, though touch'd thus faintly, are drawn right,"

I shall have nothing left to wish.

Poetry is treated in as cursory a manner as Philosophy, though not precisely for the same reasons. I have been deterred from a further developement of her nature and principles, by observing that no single subject has employed the didactic pen with such frequent success, and by a consequent unwillingness to incur a charge of tediousness, when repeating what is well known, or one of presumption, when intruding new-fangled maxims in the place of those deservedly established. The act of white-washing an ancient Gothic edifice would be less indicative of bad taste than the latter attempt. Since the time of Horace, many excellent didactic writers have formed poetic systems from detached passages of that unsystematic work, his 'Ars Poetica.' Pope, and Boileau, in their Essays on Poetry and Criticism have with superior method traced his footsteps. And yet, "haud passibus æquis"—it is only justice to observe, that though the poem has been excelled, the Poet remains unequalled. For the merits of his imitators are, except in arrangement, Horace's merits, while the merits of Horace are his own.*

I wish that the sublime circuit of intellect, embraced by the plan of my Poem, had fallen to the lot of a spirit more powerful than mine. I wish it had fallen to the lot of one familiar with the dwelling-place of Mind, who could search her secret chambers, and call forth those that sleep; or of one who could enter into her temples, and cast out the iniquitous who buy and sell, profaning the sanctuary of God; or of one who could try the golden links of that chain which hangs from Heaven to earth,

* He is indebted to Aristotle, which however cannot be said to affect his poetical originality.

and shew that it is not placed there for man to covet for lucre's sake, or for him to weigh his puny strength at one end against Omnipotence at the other; but that it is placed there to join, in mysterious union, the natural and the spiritual, the mortal and the eternal, the creature and the Creator. I wish the subject of my Poem had fallen into such hands, that the powers of the execution might have equalled the vastness of the design—and the Public will wish so too. But as it is—though I desire this field to be more meritoriously occupied by others—I would mitigate the voice of censure for myself. I would endeavour to shew, that while I may have often erred, I have not clung willingly to error; and that while I may have failed in representing, I have never ceased to love Truth. If there be much to condemn in the following pages, let my narrow capacity, as opposed to the infinite object it would embrace, be generously considered; if there be any thing to approve, I am ready to acknowledge the assistance which my illustrations have received from the exalting nature of their subject—as the waters of Halys acquire a peculiar taste from the soil over which they flow.

CONTENTS.

AN

ESSAY ON MIND.

BOOK I.

"My narrow leaves cannot in them contayne
The large discourse."—SPENSER.

Analysis of the First Book.

THE poem commences by remarking the desire, natural to the mind, of investigating its own qualities—qualities the more exalted, as their developement has seldom been impeded by external circumstances—The various dispositions of different minds are next considered, and are compared to the varieties of scenic nature: inequalities in the spiritual not being more wonderful than inequalities in the natural—Byron and Campbell contrasted—The varieties of genius having been thus treated, the art of criticism is briefly alluded to, as generally independent of genius, but always useful to its productions—Jeffrey—The various stages of life in which genius appears, and the different causes by which its influence is discovered—Cowley, Alfieri—Allusion to the story of the emotion of Thucydides on hearing Herodotus recite his History at the Olympic Games—The elements of Mind are thus arranged, Invention, Judgment, Memory, and Association—The creations of mind are next noticed, among which we first behold Philosophy—History, Science, and Metaphysics, are included in the studies of Philosophy.

Of History, it is observed, that though on a cursory view her task of recalling the past may appear of little avail, it is in reality one of the highest importance—The living are sent for a lesson to the grave—The present state of Rome alluded to; and the future state of England anticipated—Condemnation of those who deprive historical facts of their moral inference, and only make use of their basis to render falsehood more secure—Gibbon—Condemnation of those who would colour the political conduct of past ages with their own political feelings—Hume, Mitford—From the writers, we turn to the readers of history—Their extreme scepticism, or credulity—They are recommended to be guided by no faction; but to measure facts by their consistency with reason—to study the personal character and circumstances of an historian before they give entire credit to his representations—The influence of private feeling and prejudice—Miller—Science is introduced—Apostrophe to man—Episode of Archimedes—Parallel between history and science—The pride of the latter considered most excessive—The risk attending knowledge—Buffon, Leibnitz—The advantageous experience to be derived from the errors of others, illustrated by an allusion to Southey's Hexameters—Utility the object of science—An exclusive attention to parts deprecated, since it is impossible even to have a just idea of PARTS, without acquiring a knowledge of their relative situation in the whole—The extreme difficulty of enlarging the contemplations of a mind long accustomed to contracted views—The scale of knowledge—every science being linked with the one preceding and succeeding—giving and receiving reciprocal support—Why this system is not calculated, as might be conjectured, either to render scientific men superficial, or to intrude on the operations of genius—That the danger of knowledge originates in PARTIAL knowledge—Apostrophe to Newton.

ESSAY ON MIND.

BOOK I.

SINCE Spirit first inspir'd, pervaded all,
And Mind met Matter, at th' Eternal call—
Since dust weigh'd Genius down, or Genius gave
Th' immortal halo to the mortal's grave;
Th' ambitious soul her essence hath defin'd,
And Mind hath eulogiz'd the pow'rs of Mind.
Ere Revelation's holy light began
To strengthen Nature, and illumine Man—
When Genius, on Icarian pinions, flew,
And Nature's pencil, Nature's portrait, drew;

When Reason shudder'd at her own wan beam,
And Hope turn'd pale beneath the sickly gleam—
Ev'n then hath Mind's triumphant influence spoke,
Dust own'd the spell, and Plato's spirit woke—
Spread her eternal wings, and rose sublime
Beyond th' expanse of circumstance and time :
Blinded, but free, with faith instinctive, soar'd,
And found her home, where prostrate saints ador'd !

Thou thing of light ! that warm'st the breasts of man,
Breath'st from the lips, and tremblest from the pen !
Thou, form'd at once t' astonish, fire, beguile,—
With Bacon reason, and with Shakespeare smile !
The subtle cause, ethereal essence ! say,
Why dust rules dust, and clay surpasses clay ;
Why a like mass of atoms should combine
To form a Tully, and a Catiline ?

Or why, with flesh perchance of equal weight,
One cheers a prize-fight, and one frees a state?
Why do not I the muse of Homer call,
Or why, indeed, did Homer sing at all?
Why wrote not Blackstone upon love's delusion,
Or Moore, a libel on the Constitution?
Why must the faithful page refuse to tell
That Dante, Laura sang, and Petrarch, Hell—
That Tom Paine argued in the throne's defence—
That Byron nonsense wrote, and Thurlow sense—
That Southey sigh'd with all a patriot's cares,
While Locke gave utterance to Hexameters?
Thou thing of light! instruct my pen to find
Th' unequal pow'rs, the various forms of Mind!

O'er Nature's changeful face direct your sight;
View light meet shade, and shade dissolve in light!

Mark, from the plain, the cloud-capp'd mountain soar;
The sullen ocean spurn the desert shore!
Behold, afar, the playmate of the storm,
Wild Niagara lifts his awful form—
Spits his black foam above the madd'ning floods,
Himself the savage of his native woods—
See him, in air, his smoking torrents wheel,
While the rocks totter, and the forests reel—
Then, giddy, turn! lo! Shakespeare's Avon flows,
Charm'd, by the green-sward's kiss, to soft repose;
With tranquil brow reflects the smile of fame,
And, 'midst her sedges, sighs her Poet's name.

Thus, in bright sunshine, and alternate storms,
Is various mind express'd in various forms.
In equal men, why burns not equal fire?
Why are not valleys hills,—or mountains higher?

Her destin'd way, hath destin'd Nature trod ;
While Matter, Spirit rules, and Spirit, God.

Let outward scenes, for inward sense design'd,
Call back our wand'rings to the world of Mind !
Where Reason, o'er her vasty realms, may stand,
Convene proud thoughts, and stretch her scepter'd
hand.
Here, classic recollections breathe around ;
Here, living Glory consecrates the ground ;
And here, Mortality's deep waters span
The shores of Genius, and the paths of Man !

O'er this imagin'd land, your soul direct—
Mark Byron, the Mont Blanc of intellect,
'Twixt earth and heav'n exalt his brow sublime,
O'erlook the nations, and shake hands with Time !

Stretch'd at his feet do Nature's beauties throng,
The flow'rs of love, the gentleness of song;
Above, the Avalanche's thunder speaks,
While Terror's spirit walks abroad, and shrieks!
To some Utopian strand, some fairy shore,
Shall soft-eyed Fancy waft her Campbell o'er!
Wont, o'er the lyre of Hope, his hand to fling,
And never waken a discordant string;
Who ne'er grows awkward by affecting grace,
Or 'Common sense confounds with common-place;'
To bright conception, adds expression chaste,
And human feeling joins to classic taste.
For still, with magic art, he knows, and knew,
To touch the heart, and win the judgment too!

Thus, in uncertain radiance, Genius glows,
And fitful gleams on various mind bestows:

While Mind, exulting in th' admitted day,
On various themes, reflects its kindling ray.
Unequal forms receive an equal light;
And Klopstock wrote what Kepler could not write.

Yet Fame hath welcom'd a less noble few,
And Glory hail'd whom Genius never knew;
Art labour'd, Nature's birthright, to secure,
And forg'd, with cunning hand, her signature.
The scale of life is link'd by close degrees;
Motes float in sunbeams, mites exist in cheese;
Critics seize half the fame which bards receive,—
And Shakespeare suffers that his friends may live;
While Bentley leaves, on stilts, the beaten track,
And peeps at glory from some ancient's back. (*a*)
But, though to hold a lantern to the sun
Be not too wise, and were as well undone—

Though, e'en in this inventive age, alas!
A moral darkness can't be cur'd by gas—
And, though we may not reasonably deem
How poets' craniums can be turn'd by steam—
Yet own we, in our juster reasonings,
That lanterns, gas, and steam, are useful things—
And oft, this truth, Reflection ponders o'er—
Bards would write worse, if critics wrote no more.

Let Jeffrey's praise, our willing pen, engage,
The letter'd critic of a letter'd age!
Who justly judges, rightfully discerns,
With wisdom teaches, and with candour learns.
His name on Scotia's brightest tablet lives,
And proudly claims the laurel that it gives.

Eternal Genius! fashion'd like the sun,
To make all beautiful thou look'st upon!

Prometheus of our earth! whose kindling smile
May warm the things of clay a little while;
Till, by thy touch inspir'd, thine eyes survey'd,
Thou stoop'st to love the glory thou hast made;
And weepest, human-like, the mortal's fall,
When, by-and-bye, a breath disperses all.
Eternal Genius! mystic essence! say,
How, on "the chosen breast," descends thy day!
Breaks it at once in Thought's celestial dream,
While Nature trembles at the sudden gleam?
Or steals it, gently, like the morning's light,
Shedding, unmark'd, an influence soft and bright,
Till all the landscape gather on the sight?

As different talents, different breasts, inspire,
So different causes wake the latent fire.
The gentle Cowley of our native clime, (*b*)
Lisp'd his first accents in Aönian rhyme.

Alfieri's startling muse tun'd not her strings, (*c*)
And dumbly look'd "unutterable things;"
Till, when six lustrums o'er his head had past,
Conception found expression's voice at last;
Broke the bright light, uprose the smother'd flame,—
And Mind and Nature own'd their poet's fame!
To some the waving woods, the harp of spring,
A gently-breathing inspiration bring!
Some hear, from Nature's haunts, her whisper'd call;
And Mind hath triumph'd by an apple's fall.

Wave Fancy's picturing wand! recall the scene
Which Mind hath hallow'd—where her sons have been—
Where, 'midst Olympia's concourse, simply great,
Th' historic sage, the son of Lyxes, sate,
Grasping th' immortal scroll—he breath'd no sound,
But, calm in strength, an instant look'd around,

And rose—the tone of expectation rush'd
Through th' eager throng—he spake, and Greece was
hush'd !
See, in that breathless crowd, Olorus stand, (*d*)
While one fair boy hangs, list'ning, on his hand—
The young Thucydides ! with upward brow
Of radiance, and dark eye, that beaming now
Full on the speaker, drinks th' inspirëd air—
Gazing entranc'd, and turn'd to marble there !
Yet not to marble—for the wild emotion
Is kindling on his cheek, like light on ocean,
Coming to vanish ; and his pulses throb
With transport, and the inarticulate sob
Swells to his lip—internal nature leaps
To glorious life, and all th' historian weeps !
The mighty master mark'd the favor'd child—
Did Genius linger there ? She did, and smil'd !

Still, on itself, let Mind its eye direct,
To view the elements of intellect—
How wild Invention (daring artist!) plies
Her magic pencil, and creating dies;
And Judgment, near the living canvass, stands,
To blend the colours for her airy hands;
While Memory waits, with twilight mists o'ercast,
To mete the length'ning shadows of the past:
And bold Association, not untaught,
The links of fact, unites, with links of thought;
Forming th' electric chains, which, mystic, bind
Scholastic learning, and reflective mind.

Let reasoning Truth's unerring glance survey
The fair creations of the mental ray;
Her holy lips, with just discernment, teach
The forms, the attributes, the modes of each;

And tell, in simple words, the narrow span
That circles intellect, and fetters man;
Where darkling mists, o'er Time's last footstep, creep,
And Genius drops her languid wing—to weep.

See first Philosophy's mild spirit, nigh,
Raise the rapt brow, and lift the thoughtful eye;
Whether the glimmering lamp, that Hist'ry gave,
Light her enduring steps to some lone grave;
The while she dreams on him, asleep beneath,
And conjures mystic thoughts of life and death—
Whether, on Science' rushing wings, she sweep
From concave heav'n to earth—and search the deep;
Shewing the pensile globe attraction's force,
The tides their mistress, and the stars their course:
Or whether (task with nobler object fraught)
She turn the pow'rs of thinking back on thought—

With mind, delineate mind ; and dare define
The point, where human mingles with divine :
Majestic still, her solemn form shall stand,
To shew the beacon on the distant land—
Of thought, and nature, chronicler sublime !
The world her lesson, and her teacher Time !

And when, with half a smile, and half a sigh,
She lifts old History's faded tapestry,
I' the dwelling of past years—she, aye, is seen
Point to the shades, where bright'ning tints had been—
The shapeless forms outworn, and mildew'd o'er—
And bids us rev'rence what was lov'd before ;
Gives the dank wreath and dusty urn to fame,
And lends its ashes—all she can—a name.
Think'st thou, in vain, while pale Time glides away,
She rakes cold graves, and chronicles their clay ?

Think'st thou, in vain, she counts the boney things,
Once lov'd as patriots, or obey'd as kings?
Lifts she, in vain, the past's mysterious veil?
Seest thou no moral in her awful tale?
Can man, the crumbling pile of nations, scan,—
And is their mystic language mute for man?

Go! let the tomb its silent lesson give,
And let the dead instruct thee how to live!
If Tully's page hath bade thy spirit burn,
And lit the raptur'd cheek—behold his urn!
If Maro's strains, thy soaring fancy, guide,
That hail 'th' eternal city' in their pride—(*e*)
Then turn to mark, in some reflective hour,
The immortality of mortal pow'r!
See the crush'd column, and the ruin'd dome—
'Tis all Eternity has left of Rome!

While travell'd crowds, with curious gaze, repair,
To read the littleness of greatness there!

Alas! alas! so, Albion shall decay,
And all my country's glory pass away!
So shall she perish, as the mighty must,
And be Italia's rival—in the dust;
While her ennobled sons, her cities fair,
Be dimly thought of 'midst the things that were!
Alas! alas! her fields of pleasant green,
Her woods of beauty, and each well-known scene!
Soon, o'er her plains, shall grisly Ruin haste,
And the gay vale become the silent waste!
Ah! soon perchance, our native tongue forgot—
The land may hear strange words it knoweth not;
And the dear accents which our bosoms move,
With sounds of friendship, or with tones of love,

May pass away; or, conn'd on mould'ring page,
Gleam 'neath the midnight lamp, for unborn sage;
To tell our dream-like tale to future years,
And wake th' historian's smile, and schoolboy's tears!

Majestic task! to join, though plac'd afar,
The things that have been, with the things that are!
Important trust! the awful dead, to scan,
And teach mankind to moralize from man!
Stupendous charge! when, on the record true,
Depend the dead, and hang the living too!
And, oh! thrice impious he, who dares abuse
That solemn charge, and good and ill confuse!
Thrice guilty he who, false with "words of sooth,"
Would pay, to Prejudice, his debt to Truth;
The hallow'd page of fleeting Time prophane,
And prove to Man that man has liv'd in vain;

Pass the cold grave, with colder jestings, by;
And use the truth to illustrate a lie!

Let Gibbon's name be trac'd, in sorrow, here,—
Too great to spurn, too little to revere!
Who follow'd Reason, yet forgot her laws,
And found all causes, but the 'great first Cause:'
The paths of time, with guideless footsteps, trod;
Blind to the light of nature and of God;
Deaf to the voice, amid the past's dread hour,
Which sounds His praise, and chronicles His pow'r!
In vain for *him* was Truth's fair tablet spread,
When Prejudice, with jaundiced organs, read.
In vain for *us* the polish'd periods flow,
The fancy kindles, and the pages glow;
When one bright hour, and startling transport past,
The musing soul must turn—to sigh at last.

Still let the page be luminous and just,
Nor private feeling war with public trust;
Still let the pen from narrowing views forbear,
And modern faction ancient freedom spare.
But, ah! too oft th' historian bends his mind
To flatter party—not to serve mankind;
To make the dead, in living feuds, engage,
And give all time, the feelings of his age.
Great Hume hath stoop'd, the Stuarts' fame, t' increase;
And ultra Mitford soar'd to libel Greece! (*j*)

Yet must the candid muse, impartial, learn
To trace the errors which her eyes discern;
View ev'ry side, investigate each part,
And get the holy scroll of Truth by heart;
No blame misplac'd, and yet no fault forgot—
Like ink employ'd to write with—not to blot.

Hence, while historians, just reproof, incur,
We find some readers, with their authors, err ;
And soon discover, that as few excel
In reading justly, as in writing well.
For prejudice, or ignorance, is such,
That men believe too little, or too much ;
Too apt to cavil, or too glad to trust,
With confidence misplac'd, or blame unjust.

Seek out no faction—no peculiar school—
But lean on Reason, as your safest rule. (*g*)
Let doubtful facts, with patient hand, be led,
To take their place on this Procrustian bed !
What, plainly, fits not, may be thrown aside,
Without the censure of pedantic pride :
For nature still, to just proportion, clings ;
And human reason judges natural things.

Moreover, in th' historian's bosom look,
And weigh his feelings ere you trust his book;
His private friendships, private wrongs, descry,
Where tend his passions, where his int'rests lie—
And, while his proper faults your mind engage,
Discern the ruling foibles of his age.
Hence, when on deep research, the work you find
A too obtrusive transcript of his mind;
When you perceive a fact too highly wrought,
Which kindly seems to prove a fav'rite thought;
Or some opposing truth trac'd briefly out,
With hand of careless speed—then turn to doubt!
For private feeling, like the taper, glows,
And here a light, and there a shadow, throws.

If some gay picture, vilely daubed, were seen
With grass of azure, and a sky of green,

Th' impatient laughter we'd suppress in vain,
And deem the painter jesting, or insane.
But, when the sun of blinding prejudice
Glares in our faces, it deceives our eyes;
Truth appears falsehood to the dazzled sight,
The comment apes the fact, and black seems white;
Commingled hues, their separate colours lost,
Dance wildly on, in bright confusion tost;
And, midst their drunken whirl, the giddy eye
Beholds one shapeless blot for earth and sky.

Of such delusions let the mind take heed,
And learn to think, or wisely cease to read;
And, if a style of labour'd grace display
Perverted feelings, in a pleasing way;
False tints, on real objects, brightly laid,
Facts in disguise, and Truth in masquerade—

If cheating thoughts in beauteous dress appear,
With magic sound, to captivate the ear—
Th' enchanting poison of that page decline,
Or drink Circean draughts—and turn to swine!

We hail with British pride, and ready praise,
Enlightened Miller of our modern days! (*h*)
Too firm though temp'rate, liberal though exact,
To give too much to argument or fact,
To love details, and draw no moral thence,
Or seek the comment, and forget the sense,
He leaves all vulgar aims, and strives alone
To find the ways of Truth, and make them known!

Spirit of life! for aye, with heav'nly breath,
Warm the dull clay, and cold abodes of death!
Clasp in its urn the consecrated dust,
And bind a laurel round the broken bust;

While mid decaying tombs, thy pensive choice,
Thou bidst the silent utter forth a voice,
To prompt the actors of our busy scene,
And tell what *is*, the tale of what *has been !*

Yet turn, Philosophy ! with brow sublime,
Shall Science follow on the steps of Time !
As, o'er Thought's measureless depths, we bend to hear
The whispered sound, which stole on Descartes' ear, (*i*)
Hallowing the sunny visions of his youth
With that eternal mandate, "Search for Truth !"
Yes ! search for Truth—the glorious path is free;
Mind shews her dwelling—Nature holds the key—
Yes ! search for Truth—her tongue shall bid thee scan
The book of knowledge, for the use of Man !

Man ! Man ! thou poor antithesis of power !
Child of all time ! yet creature of an hour !

By turns, camelion of a thousand forms,
The lord of empires, and the food of worms!
The little conqueror of a petty space,
The more than mighty, or the worse than base!
Thou ruin'd landmark, in the desert way,
Betwixt the all of glory, and decay!
Fair beams the torch of Science in thine hand,
And sheds its brightness o'er the glimmering land;
While, in thy native grandeur, bold, and free,
Thou bid'st the wilds of nature smile for thee,
And treadest Ocean's paths full royally!
Earth yields her treasures up—celestial air
Receives thy globe of life—when, journeying there,
It bounds from dust, and bends its course on high,
And walks, in beauty, through the wondering sky.
And yet, proud clay! thine empire is a span,
Nor all thy greatness makes thee more than man!

While Knowledge, Science, only serve t' impart
The god thou *would'st* be, and the thing thou *art!*

Where stands the Syracusan—while the roar
Of men, and engines, echoes through the shore?
Where stands the Syracusan? haggard Fate,
With ghastly smile, is sitting at the gate;
And Death forgets his silence 'midst the crash
Of rushing ruins—and the torches' flash
Waves redly on the straggling forms that die;
And masterless steeds, beneath that gleam, dart by,
Scared into madness, by the battle cry—
And sounds are hurtling in the angry air,
Of hate, and pain, and vengeance, and despair—
The smothered voice of babes—the long wild shriek
Of mothers—and the curse the dying speak!

Where stands the Syracusan? tranquil sage,
He bends, sublime, o'er Science' splendid page;
Walks the high circuit of extended mind,
Surpasses man, and dreams not of mankind;
While, on his listless ear, the battle shout
Falls senseless—as if echo breath'd about
The hum of many words, the laughing glee,
Which linger'd there, when Syracuse was free.
Away! away! for louder accents fall—
But not the sounds of joy from marble hall!
Quick steps approach—but not of sylphic feet,
Whose echo heralded a smile more sweet,
Coming, all sport, th' indulgent sage, t' upbraid
For lonely hours, to studious musing, paid—
Be hushed! Destruction bares the flickering blade!
He asked to live, th' unfinished lines to fill,
And died—to solve a problem deeper still.

He died, the glorious! who, with soaring sight, (*j*)
Sought some new world, to plant his foot of might;
Thereon, in solitary pride, to stand,
And lift our planet, with a master's hand!
He sank in death—Creation only gave
That thorn-encumbered space which forms his grave—
An unknown grave, till Tully chanced to stray,
And named the spot where Archimedes lay!
Genius! behold the limit of thy power!
Thou fir'st the soul—but, when life's dream is o'er,
Giv'st not the silent pulse one throb the more:
And mighty beings come, and pass away,
Like other comets, and like other—clay.

Though analyzing Truth must still divide
Historic state, and scientific pride;
Yet one stale fact, our judging thoughts infer—
Since each is human, each is prone to err!

Oft, in the night of Time, doth History stray,
And lift her lantern, and proclaim it day!
And oft, when day's eternal glories shine,
Doth Science, boasting, cry—"The light is mine!"
So hard to bear, with unobstructed sight, (*k*)
Th' excess of darkness, or th' extreme of light.

Yet, to be just, though faults belong to each,
The themes of one, an humbler moral, teach:
And, 'midst th' historian's eloquence, and skill,
The human chronicler is human still.
If on past power, his eager thoughts be cast,
It brings an awful antidote—'tis past!
If, deathless fame, his ravish'd organs scan,
The deathless fame exists for buried man:
Power, and decay, at once he turns to view;
And, with the strength, beholds the weakness too.

Not so, doth Science' musing son aspire ;
And pierce creation, with his eye of fire.
Yon mystic pilgrims of the starry way,
No humbling lesson, to his soul, convey;
No tale of change, their changeless course hath taught;
And works divine excite no earthward thought.
And still, he, reckless, builds the splendid dream ;
And still, his pride increases with his theme ;
And still, the cause is slighted in th' effect ;
And still, self-worship follows self-respect.
Too apt to watch the engines of the scene,
And lose the hand, which moves the vast machine ;
View Matter's form, and not its moving soul ;
Interpret parts, and misconceive the whole :
While, darkly musing 'twixt the earth, and sky,
His heart grows narrow, as his hopes grow high ;
And quits, for aye, with unavailing loss,
The sympathies of earth, but not the dross ;

Till Time sweeps down the fabric of his trust;
And life, and riches, turn to death, and dust.

And such is Man! 'neath Error's foul assaults,
His noblest moods beget his grossest faults!
When Knowledge lifts her hues of varied grace,
The fair exotic of a brighter place,
To keep her stem, from mundane blasts, enshrin'd,
He makes a fatal hot-bed of his mind;
Too oft adapted, in their growth, to spoil
The natural beauties of a generous soil.
Ah! such is Man! thus strong, and weak withal,
His rise oft renders him too prone to fall!
The loftiest hills' fresh tints, the soonest, fade;
And highest buildings cast the deepest shade!

So Buffon err'd; amidst his chilling dream, (*l*)
The judgment grew material as the theme:

Musing on Matter, till he called away
The modes of Mind, to form the modes of clay ;
And made, confusing each, with judgment blind,
Mind stoop to dust, and dust ascend to Mind.
So Leibnitz err'd ; when, in the starry hour,
He read no weakness, where was written, 'Power ;'
Beheld the verdant earth, the circling sea ;
Nor dreamt so fair a world could cease to be !
Yea ! but he heard the Briton's awful name,
As, scattering darkness, in his might, he came,
Girded with Truth, and earnest to confute
What gave to Matter, Mind's best attribute.
Sternly they strove—th' unequal race was run ! (*m*)
The owlet met the eagle at the sun !

While such defects, their various forms, unfold ;
And rust, so foul, obscures the brightest gold—

Let Science' soaring sons, the ballast, cast,
But judge their present errors, by their past.
As some poor wanderer, in the darkness, goes,
When fitful wind, in hollow murmur, blows;
Hailing, with trembling joy, the lightning's ray,
Which threats his safety, but illumes his way.

Gross faults buy deep experience. Sages tell
That Truth, like Æsop's fox, is in a well;
And, like the goat, his fable prates about,
Fools must stay in, that wise men may get out.
What thousand scribblers, of our age, would choose
To throw a toga round the English muse;
Rending her garb of ease, which graceful grew
From Dryden's loom, beprankt with varied hue!
In that dull aim, by Mind unsanctified,
What thousand Wits would have their wits belied,
Devoted Southey! if thou had'st not tried! (*n*)

Use is the aim of Science; this the end
The wise appreciate, and the good commend.
For not, like babes, the flaming torch, we prize,
That sparkling lustre may attract our eyes;
But that, when evening shades impede the sight,
It casts, on objects round, a useful light.

Use is the aim of Science! give again
A golden sentence to the faithful pen—
Dwell not on parts! for parts contract the mind; (*o*)
And knowledge still is useless, when confined.
The yearning soul, inclosed in narrow bound,
May be ingenious, but is ne'er profound:
Spoil'd of its strength, the fettered thought grows tame;
And want of air extinguishes the flame!
And as the sun, beheld in mid-day blaze,
Seems turned to darkness, as we strive to gaze;

So mental vigour, on one object, cast,
That object's self becomes obscured at last.

'Tis easy, as Experience may aver,
To pass from general to particular.
But most laborious to direct the soul
From studying parts, to reason on the whole :
Thoughts, train'd on narrow subjects, to let fall ;
And learn the unison of each with all.

In Nature's reign, a scale of life, we find:
A scale of knowledge, we behold, in mind ;
With each progressive link, our steps ascend,
And traverse all, before they reach the end ;
Searching, while Reason's powers may farther go,
The things we know not, by the things we know.

But hold ! methinks some sons of Thought demand,
"Why strive to form the Trajan's vase in sand ?
Are Reason's paths so few, that Mind may call
Her finite energies, to tread them all ?
Lo ! Learning's waves, in bounded channel, sweep ;
When they flow wider, shall they run as deep ?
Shall that broad surface, no dull shallow, hide,
Growing dank weeds of superficial pride ?
Then Heaven may leave our giant powers alone ;
Nor give each soul a focus of its own !
Genius bestows, in vain, the chosen page,
If all the tome, the minds of all, engage !"

Nay ! I reply—with free congenial breast,
Let each peruse the part, which suits him best !
But, lest contracting prejudice mislead,
Regard the context, as he turns to read !

Hence, liberal feeling gives th' enlighten'd soul,
The spirit, with the letter of the scroll.

With what triumphant joy, what glad surprise,
The dull behold the dulness of the wise!
What insect tribes of brainless impudence
Buzz round the carcase of perverted sense!
What railing ideots hunt, from classic school,
Each flimsy sage, and scientific fool,
Crying, "'Tis well! we see the blest effect
Of watchful night, and toiling intellect!"
Yet let them pause, and tremble—vainly glad;
For too much learning maketh no man mad! (*p*)
Too *little* dims the sight, and leads us o'er
The twilight path, where fools have been before;
With not enough of Reason's radiance seen,
To track the footsteps, where those fools have been.

Divinest Newton! if my pen may shew
A name so mighty, in a verse so low,—
Still let the sons of Science, joyful, claim
The bright example of that splendid name!
Still let their lips repeat, my page bespeak,
The sage how learned! and the man how meek! (*q*)
Too wise, to think his human folly less;
Too great, to doubt his proper littleness;
Too strong, to deem his weakness past away;
Too high in soul, to glory in his clay:
Rich in all nature, but her erring side:
Endow'd with all of Science—but its pride.

AN

ESSAY ON MIND.

BOOK II.

Analysis of the Second Book.

METAPHYSICS—Addresss to Metaphysicians—The most considerable portion of their errors conceived to arise from difficulties attending the use of words—That on one hand, thoughts become obscure without the assistance of language, while on the other, language from its material analogy deteriorates from spiritual meaning—Allusion to a probable mode of communication between spirits after death—That a limited respect, though not a servile submission, is due to verbal distinctions—Clearness of style peculiarly necessary to Metaphysical subjects—The graces of Composition not inconsistent with them—Plato, Bacon, Bolingbroke—The extremes into which Philosophers have fallen with regard to sensation, and reflection—Berkeley, Condillac—That subject briefly considered—Abstractions—Longinus, Burke, Price, Payne Knight—Blind submission to authorities deprecated—The Pythagorean saying opposed, and Cicero's unphilosophical assertion alluded to—That, however, it partakes of injustice to love Truth, and yet refuse our homage to the advocates of Truth—How the names of great writers become endeared to us by early recollections—Description of the School-boy's first intellectual gratifications—That even without reference to the past, some immortal names are entitled to our veneration, since they are connected with Truth—Bacon—Apostrophe to Locke.

Poetry is introduced—More daring than Philosophy, she personifies abstractions, and brings the things unseen before the eye of the Mind—How often reason is indebted to poetic imagery—Irving—The poetry of prose—Plato's ingratitude—Philosophers and Poets contrasted—An attempt to define Poetry—That the passions make use of her language—Nature the poet's study—Shakspeare—Human nature as seen in cities—Scenic nature, and how the mind is affected thereby—That Poetry exists not in the object contemplated, but is created by the contemplating mind—The ideal—Observations on the structure of verse, as adapted to the subject treated—Milton, Horace, Pope—The French Drama—Corneille, Racine—Harmony and chasteness of versification—The poem proceeds to argue, that the muse will refuse her inspiration to a soul unattuned to generous sympathy, unkindled by the deeds of Virtue, or the voice of Freedom—Contemptuous notice of those prompted only by interest to aspire to poetic eminence—What should be the Poet's best guerdon—From the contemplation of motives connected with Freedom, we are led by no unnatural transition to Greece—Her present glorious struggle—Anticipation of her ultimate independence, and the restoration of the Muses to their ancient seats—Allusion to the death of Byron—Reflections on Mortality—The terrors of death as beheld by the light of Nature—The consolations of death as beheld with reference to a future state—Contemplation of the immortality of Mind, and her perfected powers—Conclusion.

ESSAY ON MIND.

BOOK II.

BUT now to higher themes! no more confin'd
To copy Nature, Mind returns to Mind.
We leave the throng, so nobly, and so well,
Tracing, in Wisdom's book, things visible,—
And turn to things unseen; where, greatly wrought,
Soul questions soul, and thought revolves on thought.
My spirit loves, my voice shall hail ye, now,
Sons of the patient eye, and passionless brow!
Students sublime! Earth, man, unmov'd, ye view,
Time, circumstance; for what are they to you?

What is the crash of worlds,—the fall of kings,—
When worlds and monarchs are such brittle things!
What the tost, shatter'd bark, that blindly dares
A sea of storm? Ye sketch the wave which bears!
The cause, and not th' effect, your thoughts exact;
The principle of action, not the act,—
The soul! the soul! and, 'midst so grand a task,
Ye call her rushing passions, and ye ask
Whence are ye? and each mystic thing responds!
I would be all *ye* are—except those bonds!

Except those bonds! ev'n here is oft descried
The love to parts, the poverty of pride!
Ev'n here, while Mind, in Mind's horizon, springs,
Her "native mud" is weighing on her wings!
Ev'n here, while Truth invites the ardent crowd,
Ixion-like, they rush t' embrace a cloud!

Ev'n here, oh! foul reproach to human wit!
A Hobbes hath reasoned, and Spinosa writ!

Rank pride does much! and yet we justly cry,
Our greatest errors in our weakness lie.
For thoughts uncloth'd by language are, at best,
Obscure; while grossness injures those exprest—
Through words,—in whose analysis, we find
Th' analogies of Matter, not of Mind:
Hence, when the use of words is graceful brought,
As physical dress to metaphysic thought,
The thought, howe'er sublime its pristine state,
Is by th' expression made degenerate;
Its spiritual essence changed, or cramp'd; and hence
Some hold by words, who cannot hold by sense;
And leave the thought behind, and take th' attire—
Elijah's mantle—but without his fire!

Yet spurn not words! 'tis needful to confess
They give ideas, a body and a dress!
Behold them traverse Learning's region round,
The vehicles of thought on wheels of sound;
Mind's winged strength, wherewith the height is won,
Unless she trust their frailty to the sun.
Destroy the body!—will the spirit stay?
Destroy the car!—will Thought pursue her way?
Destroy the wings!—let Mind their aid forego!
Do no Icarian billows yawn below?
Ah! spurn not words with reckless insolence;
But still admit their influence with the sense,
And fear to slight their laws! Perchance we find
No perfect code transmitted to mankind;
And yet mankind, till life's dark sands are run,
Prefers imperfect government to none.

Thus Thought must bend to words!—Some sphere
of bliss,
Ere long, shall free her from th' alloy of this:
Some kindred home for Mind—some holy place,
Where spirits look on spirits, "face to face,"—
Where souls may see, as they themselves are seen,
And voiceless intercourse may pass between,
All pure—all free! as light, which doth appear
In its own essence, incorrupt and clear!
One service, praise! one age, eternal youth!
One tongue, intelligence! one subject, truth!

Till then, no freedom, Learning's search affords,
Of soul from body, or of thought from words.
For thought may lose, in struggling to be hence,
The gravitating power of Common-sense;
Through all the depths of space with Phaeton hurl'd,
T' impair our reason, as he scorch'd our world.

Hence, this preceptive truth, my page affirms—
Respect the technicality of terms!
Yet not in base submission—lest we find
That, aiding clay, we crouch too low for Mind;
Too apt conception's essence to forget,
And place all wisdom in the alphabet.

Still let appropriate phrase the sense invest;
That what is well conceived be well exprest!
Nor e'er the reader's wearied brain engage,
In hunting meaning down the mazy page,
With three long periods tortured into one,
The sentence ended, with the sense begun;
Nor in details, which schoolboys know by heart,
Perplex each turning with the terms of art.
To understand, we deem no common good;
And 'tis less easy to be *understood.*

But let not clearness be your only praise,
When style may charm a thousand different ways;
In Plato glow, to life and glory wrought,
By high companionship with noblest thought;
In Bacon, warm abstraction with a breath,
Catch Poesy's bright beams, and smile beneath;
In St. John roll, a generous stream, along,
Correctly free, and regularly strong.
Nor scornful deem the effort out of place,
With taste to reason, and convince with grace;
But ponder wisely, ere you know, too late,
Contempt of trifles will not prove us great!
The Cynics, not their tubs, respect engage;
And dirty tunic never made a sage.
E'en Cato—had he own'd the Senate's will,
And wash'd his toga—had been Cato still. (*a*)

Justly we censure—yet are free to own,
That indecision is a crime unknown.
For, never faltering, seldom reasoning long,
And still most positive whene'er most wrong,
No theoretic sage is apt to fare
Like Mah'met's coffin—hung in middle air!
No! fenc'd by Error's all-sufficient trust,
These stalk "in nubibus"—those crawl in dust.
From their proud height, the first demand to know,
If spiritual essence should descend more low?
The last, as vainly, from their dunghill, cry,
Can body's grossness hope t' aspire more high?
And while Reflection's empire, these disclose,
Sensation's sovereign right is told by those.
Lo! Berkeley proves an old hypothesis!
'Out on the senses!' (he was out of his!)
'All is idea! and nothing real springs
But God, and Reason'—(not the right of kings?) (*b*)

'Hold!' says Condillac with profound surprise—
'Why prate of Reason? we have ears and eyes!'

Condillac! while the dangerous periods fall
Upon thy page, to stamp sensation *all;*
While (coldly studious!) thine ingenious scroll (*c*)
Endows the mimic statue with a soul
Compos'd of sense—behold the generous hound—
His piercing eye, his ear awake to sound,
His scent, most delicate organ! and declare
What triumph hath the "Art of thinking" there! (*d*)
What Gall, or Spurzheim, on his front hath sought,
The mystic bumps indicative of Thought?
Or why, if Thought *do* there maintain her throne,
Will reasoning curs leave logic for a bone?

Mind is imprison'd in a lonesome tower:
Sensation is its window—hence herb, flower,

Landscapes all sun, the rush of thousand springs,
Waft in sweet scents, fair sights, soft murmurings;
And in her joy, she gazeth—yet ere long,
Reason awaketh in her, bold and strong,
And o'er the scene exerting secret laws,
First seeks th' efficient, then the final cause,
Abstracts from forms their hidden accidents,
And marks in outward substance, inward sense.

Our first perceptions formed—we search, to find
The operations of the forming mind;
And turn within by Reason's certain route,
To view the shadows of the things without
Discern'd, retain'd, compar'd, combin'd, and brought
To mere abstraction, by abstracting Thought.
Hence to discern, retain, compare, connect,
We deem the faculties of Intellect;

The which, mus'd on, exert a new controul,
And fresh ideas are open'd on the soul.

Sensation is a stream with dashing spray,
That shoots in idle speed its arrowy way;
When lo! the mill arrests its waters' course,
Turning to use their unproductive force:
The cunning wheels by foamy currents sped,
Reflection triumphs,—and mankind is fed!

Since Pope hath shewn, and Learning still must shew,
'We cannot reason but from what we know,'—
Unfold the scroll of Thought; and turn to find
The undeceiving signature of Mind!
There, judge her nature by her nature's course,
And trace her actions upwards to their source.

So when the property of Mind we call
An essence, or a substance spiritual,
We name her thus, by marking how she clings
Less to the forms than essences of things;
For body clings to body—objects seen
And substance sensible alone have been
Sensation's study; while reflective Mind,
Essence unseen in objects seen may find;
And, tracing whence her known impressions came,
Give single forms an universal name.

So, when particular sounds in concord rise,
Those sounds as *melody*, we generalize;
When pleasing shapes and colours blend, the soul
Abstracts th' idea of *beauty* from the whole,
Deducting thus, by Mind's enchanting spell,
The intellectual from the sensible.

Hence bold Longinus' splendid periods grew,
'Who was himself the great sublime he drew:'
Hence Burke, the poet-reasoner, learn'd to trace
His glowing style of energetic grace:
Hence thoughts, perchance, some favour'd bosoms move,
Which Price might own, and classic Knight approve!

Go! light a rushlight, ere the day is done,
And call its glimm'ring brighter than the sun!
Go! while the stars in midnight glory beam,
Prefer their cold reflection in the stream!
But be not that dull slave, who only looks
On Reason, "through the spectacles of books!"
Rather by Truth determine what is true,—
And reasoning works, through Reason's medium, view;

For authors can't monopolize her light:
'Tis your's to read, as well as their's to write.
To judge is your's!—then why submissive call, (*e*)
'The master said so?'—'tis no rule at all!
Shall passive sufferance e'en to mind belong,
When right divine in man is human wrong?
Shall a high name a low idea enhance,
When all may fail, as some succeed—by chance?
Shall fix'd chimeras unfix'd reason shock?
And if Locke err, must thousands err with Locke?
Men! claim your charter! spurn th' unjust controul,
And shake the bondage from the free-born soul!
Go walk the porticoes! and teach your youth
All names are bubbles, but the name of Truth!
If fools, by chance, attend to Wisdom's rules,
'Tis no dishonour to be right with fools.
If human faults to Plato's page belong, (*f*)
Not ev'n with Plato, willingly go wrong.

But though the judging page declare it well
To love Truth better than the lips which tell;
Yet 'twere an error, with injustice class'd,
T' adore the former, and neglect the last.
Oh! beats there, Heav'n! a heart of human frame,
Whose pulses throb not at some kindling name?
Some sound, which brings high musings in its track,
Or calls perchance the days of childhood back,
In its dear echo,—when, without a sigh,
Swift hoop, and bounding ball, were first laid by,
To clasp in joy, from school-room tyrant, free,
The classic volume on the little knee,
And con sweet sounds of dearest minstrelsy,
Or words of sterner lore; the young brow fraught
With a calm brightness which might mimic thought,
Leant on the boyish hand—as, all the while,
A half-heav'd sigh, or aye th' unconscious smile

Would tell how, o'er that page, the soul was glowing,
In an internal transport, past the knowing!
How feelings, erst unfelt, did then appear,
Give forth a voice, and murmur, "We are here!"
As lute-strings, which a strong hand plays upon;
Or Memnon's statue singing 'neath the sun. (*g*)
Ah me! for such are pleasant memories—
And call the tears of fondness to our eyes
Reposing on this gone-by dream—when thus,
One marbled book was all the world to us;
The gentlest bliss our innocent thoughts could find—
The happiest cradle of our infant mind!
And though such hours be past, we shall not less
Think on their joy with grateful tenderness;
And bless the page which bade our reason wake,—
And love the prophet, for his mission's sake.

But not alone doth Memory's smouldering flame
Reflect a radiance on a glorious name;
For there are names of pride; and they who bear
Have walked with Truth, and turn'd their footsteps
where
We walk not—their beholdings aye have been
O'er Mind's far countries which we have not seen—
Our thoughts are not their thoughts!—and oft we
dream
That light upon the awful brow doth gleam,
From that high converse; as when Moses trod
Towards the people, from the mount of God,
His lips were silent, but his face was bright,
And prostrate Israel trembled at the sight.

What tongue can syllable our Bacon's name,
Nor own a heart exulting in his fame?

Where prejudice' wild blasts were wont to blow,
And waves of ignorance roll'd dark below,
He raised his sail—and left the coast behind,—
Sublime Columbus of the realms of Mind!
Dared folly's mists, opinion's treacherous sands,
And walk'd, with godlike step, th' untrodden lands!
But ah! our Muse of Britain, standing near, (*h*)
Hath dimm'd my tablet with a pensive tear!
Thrice, the proud theme, her free-born voice essays,—
And thrice that voice is faltering in his praise—
Yea! till her eyes in silent triumph turn
To mark afar her Locke's sepulchral urn!
Oh urn! where students rapturous vigils keep,
Where sages envy, and where patriots weep!
Oh Name! that bids my glowing spirit wake—
To freemen's hearts endeared for Freedom's sake!

Oh soul! too bright in life's corrupting hour,
To rise by faction, or to crouch to power!
While radiant Genius lifts her heav'nward wing,
And human bosoms own the Mind I sing;
While British writers British thoughts record,
And England's press is fearless as her sword;
While, 'mid the seas which gird our favor'd isle,
She clasps her charter'd rights with conscious smile;
So long be *thou* her glory, and her guide,
Thy page her study, and thy name her pride!
Oh! ever thus, immortal Locke, belong
First to my heart, as noblest in my song;
And since in thee, the muse enraptured find
A moral greatness, and creating mind,
Still may thine influence, which with honor'd light
Beams when I read, illume me as I write!

The page too guiltless, and the soul too free,
To call a frown from Truth, or blush from thee!
But where Philosophy would fear to soar,
Young Poesy's elastic steps explore!
Her fairy foot, her daring eye pursues
The light of faith—nor trembles as she views!
Wont o'er the Psalmist's holy harp to hang,
And swell the sacred note when Milton sang;
Mingling reflection's chords with fancy's lays,
The tones of music with the voice of praise!

And while Philosophy, in spirit, free,
Reasons, believes, yet cannot plainly *see*,
Poetic Rapture, to her dazzled sight,
Pourtrays the shadows of the things of light;
Delighting o'er the unseen worlds to roam,
And waft the pictures of perfection home.

Thus Reason oft the aid of fancy seeks,
And strikes Pierian chords—when Irving speaks! (*i*)

Oh! silent be the withering tongue of those
Who call each page, bereft of measure, prose;
Who deem the Muse possest of such faint spells,
That like poor fools, she glories in her *bells*;
Who hear her voice alone in tinkling chime,
And find a line's whole magic in its rhyme;
Forgetting, if the gilded shrine be fair,
What purer spirit may inhabit there!
For such,—indignant at her questioned might,
Let Genius cease to charm—and Scott to write!

Ungrateful Plato! o'er thy cradled rest, (*j*)
The Muse hath hung, and all her love exprest;

Thy first imperfect accents fondly taught,
And warm'd thy visions with poetic thought!
Ungrateful Plato! should her deadliest foe
Be found within the breast she tended so?
Spoil'd of her laurels, should she weep to find
The best belov'd become the most unkind?
And was it well or generous, Brutus like,
To pierce the hand that gave the power to strike?

Sages, by reason, reason's powers direct;
Bards, through the heart, convince the intellect.
Philosophy majestic brings to view
Mind's perfect modes, and fair proportions too;
Enchanting Poesy bestows the while,
Upon its sculptured grace, her magic smile,
Bids the cold form, with living radiance glow,
And stamps existence on its marble brow!

For Poesy's whole essence, when defined,
Is elevation of the reasoning mind,
When inward sense from Fancy's page is taught,
And moral feeling ministers to Thought.
And hence, the natural passions all agree
In seeking Nature's language—poetry.
When Hope, in soft perspective, from afar,
Sees lovely scenes more lovely than they are;
To deck the landscape, tiptoe Fancy brings
Her plastic shapes, and bright imaginings.
Or when man's breast by torturing pangs is stung,
If fearful silence cease t' enchain his tongue,
In metaphor, the feelings seek relief,
And all the soul grows eloquent with grief.

Poetic fire, like Vesta's, pure and bright,
Should draw from Nature's sun, its holy light.

With Nature, should the musing poet roam,
And steal instruction from her classic tome;
When 'neath her guidance, least inclin'd to err—
The ablest painter when he copies *her*.

Beloved Shakespeare! England's dearest fame!
Dead is the breast that swells not at thy name!
Whether thine Ariel skim the seas along,
Floating on wings etherial as his song—
Lear rave amid the tempest—or Macbeth
Question the hags of hell on midnight heath—
Immortal Shakespeare! still, thy lips impart
The noblest comment on the human heart.
And as fair Eve, in Eden newly placed, (*k*)
Gazed on her form, in limpid waters traced,
And stretch'd her gentle arms, with pleased surprise,
To meet the image of her own bright eyes—

So Nature, on thy magic page, surveys
Her sportive graces, and untutored ways!
Wondering, the soft reflection doth she see,
Then laughing owns she loves herself in thee!

Shun not the haunts of crowded cities then;
Nor e'er, as man, forget to study men!
What though the tumult of the town intrude
On the deep silence, and the lofty mood;
'Twill make thy human sympathies rejoice,
To hear the music of a human voice—
To watch strange brows by various reason wrought,
To claim the interchange of thought with thought;
T' associate mind with mind, for Mind's own weal,
As steel is ever sharpen'd best by steel.
T' impassion'd bards, the scenic world is dear,—
But Nature's glorious masterpiece is here!

All poetry is beauty, but exprest
In inward essence, not in outward vest.
Hence lovely scenes, reflective poets find,
Awake their lovelier images in Mind :
Nor doth the pictur'd earth, the bard invite,
The lake of azure, or the heav'n of light,
But that his swelling breast arouses there,
Something less visible, and much more fair !
There is a music in the landscape round,—
A silent voice, that speaks without a sound—
A witching spirit, that reposing near,
Breathes to the heart, but comes not to the ear !
These softly steal, his kindling soul t' embrace,
And natural beauty, gild with moral grace.
Think not, when summer breezes tell their tale,
The poet's thoughts are with the summer gale ;
Think not his Fancy builds her elfin dream
On painted floweret, or on sighing stream :

No single objects cause his raptured starts,
For Mind is narrow'd, not inspir'd by parts;
But o'er the scene the poet's spirit broods,
To warm the thoughts that form his noblest moods;
Peopling his solitude with faëry play,
And beckoning shapes that whisper him away,—
While lilied fields, and hedge-row blossoms white,
And hills, and glittering streams, are full in sight—
The forests wave, the joyous sun beguiles,
And all the poetry of Nature smiles!

Such poetry is formed by Mind, and not
By scenic grace of one peculiar spot.
The artist lingers in the moon-lit glade, (*l*)
And light and shade, with him, are—light and shade.
The philosophic chymist wandering there,
Dreams of the soil, and nature of the air.

The rustic marks the young herbs' fresh'ning hue,
And only thinks—his scythe may soon pass through!
None "muse on nature with a Poet's eye,"
None read, but Poets, Nature's poetry!
Its characters are trac'd in mystic hand,
And all may gaze, but few can understand.

Nor here alone the Poet's dwelling rear,
Though Beauty's voice perchance is sweetest here!
Bind not his footsteps to the sylvan scene,
To heathy banks, fair woods, and valleys green,
When Mind is all his own! her dear impress
Shall throw a magic o'er the wilderness,
As o'er the blossoming vale, and aye recall
Its shadowy plane, and silver waterfall,
Or sleepy crystal pool, reposing by,
To give the earth a picture of the sky!

Such, gazed on by the spirit, are I ween,
Lovelier than ever prototype was seen;
For Fancy teacheth Memory's hand to trace (*m*)
Nature's ideal form in Nature's place.

In every theme by lofty Poet sung,
The thought should seem to speak, and not the tongue.
When godlike Milton lifts th' exalted song,
The subject bears the burning words along—
Resounds the march of Thought, th' o'erflowing line,
Full cadence, solemn pause, and strength divine!
When Horace chats his neighbour's faults away,
The sportive measures, like his muse, are gay;
For once Good-humour Satire's by-way took,
And all his soul is laughing in his book!
On moral Pope's didactic page is found,
Sound rul'd by sense, and sense made clear by sound;

The power to reason, and the taste to please,
While, as the subject varies in degrees,
He stoops with dignity, and soars with ease.

Hence let our Poets, with discerning glance,
Forbear to imitate the stage of France.
What though Corneille arouse the thrilling chords,
And walk with Genius o'er th' inspirëd boards;
What though his rival bring, with calmer grace,
The classic unities of time and place,—
All polish, and all eloquence—'twere mean
To leave the path of Nature for Racine;
When Nero's parent, 'midst her woe, defines
The wrong that tortures—in two hundred lines:
Or when Orestes, madden'd by his crime,
Forgets life, joy, and every thing—but rhyme.

While thus to character and nature, true,
Still keep the harmony of verse in view;
Yet not in changeless concord,—it should be
Though graceful, nervous,—musical, though free;
Not clogg'd by useless drapery, not beset
By the superfluous word, or epithet,
Wherein Conception only dies in state, (*n*)
As Draco, smother'd by the garments' weight—
But join, Amphion-like, (whose magic fire
Won the deep music of the Maian lyre,
To call Bœotia's city from the ground,)
The just in structure, with the sweet in sound.

Nor this the whole—the poet's classic strain
May flow in smoothest numbers, yet in vain;
And Taste may please, and Fancy sport awhile,
And yet Aonia's muse refuse to smile!

For lo! her heavenly lips these words reveal—
'The sage may coldly *think*, the bard must *feel!*
And if his writings, to his heart untrue,
Would ape the fervent throb it never knew;
If generous deeds, and Virtue's noblest part,
And Freedom's voice, could never warm that heart;
If Interest tax'd the produce of the brain,
And fetter'd Genius follow'd in her train,
Weeping as each unwilling word she spoke,—
Then hush the lute—its master string is broke!
In vain, the skilful hand may linger o'er—
Concord is dead, and music speaks no more!'

There are, and have been such—they were forgot
If shame could veil their page, if tears could blot!
There are, and have been, whose dishonour'd lay
Aspired t' enrapture that the world might—pay!

Whose life was one long bribe, oft counted o'er,—
Brib'd to think on, and brib'd to think no more;
Brib'd to laugh, weep, nor ask the reason why;
Brib'd to tell truth, and brib'd to gild a lie!
Oh Man! for this, the sensual left behind,
We boast our empire o'er the vast of Mind?
Oh Mind! reported valueless, till sold,
Thought dross till metamorphos'd into gold
By Midas' touch—breath'st thou immortal verse
To throw a ducat in an empty purse—
To walk the market at a belman's cry,
For knaves to sell, and wond'ring fools to buy?
Can Heav'n-born bards, undone by lucre's lust,
Crouch thus, like Heav'n-born ministers, to dust?
Alas! to dust indeed—yet wherefore blame?
They keep their profits, though they lose their fame.

Leave to the dross they seek, the grovelling throng,
And swell with nobler aim th' Aonian song!
Enough for thee uninfluenc'd and unhir'd,
If Truth reward the strain herself inspir'd!
Enough for thee, if grateful Man commend,
If Genius love, and Virtue call thee friend!
Enough for thee, to wake th' exalted mood,
Reprove the erring, and confirm the good;
Excite the tender smile, the generous tear,
Or rouse the thought to loftiest Nature dear,
Which rapturous greets amidst the fervent line,
Thy name, O Freedom! glorious Hellas, thine!

I love my own dear land—it doth rejoice
The soul, to stretch my arms, and lift my voice,
To tell her of my love! I love her green,
And bowery woods, her hills in mossy sheen,

Her silver running waters—there's no spot
In all her dwelling, which my breast loves not—
No place not heart-enchanted! Sunnier skies,
And calmer waves, may meet another's eyes;
I love the sullen mist, the stormy sea,
The winds of rushing strength which, like the land,
are free!
Such is my love—yet turning thus to thee,
Oh Græcia! I must hail with hardly less
Of joy, and pride, and deepening tenderness,
And feelings wild, I know not to controul,
My other country—country of my soul!
For so, to me, thou art! my lips have sung
Of thee with childhood's lisp, and harp unstrung!
In thee, my Fancy's pleasant walks have been,
Telling her tales, while Memory wept between!
And now *for* thee I joy, with heart beguiled,
As if a dying friend looked up, and smiled.

Lo! o'er Ægæa's waves, the shout hath ris'n!
Lo! Hope hath burst the fetters of her prison!
And Glory sounds the trump along the shore,
And Freedom walks where Freedom walk'd before!
Ipsara glimmers with heroic light,
Redd'ning the waves that lash her flaming height;
And Ægypt hurries from that dark blue sea!
Lo! o'er the cliffs of fam'd Thermopylæ,
And voiceful Marathon, the wild winds sweep,
Bearing this message to the brave who sleep—
'They come! they come! with their embattled shock,
From Pelion's steep, and Paros' foam-dash'd rock!
They come from Tempe's vale, and Helicon's spring,
And proud Eurotas' banks, the river king!
They come from Leuctra, from the waves that kiss
Athena—from the shores of Salamis;
From Sparta, Thebes, Eubœa's hills of blue—
To live with Hellas—or to sleep with you!'

Smile—smile, beloved land! and though no lay
From Doric pipe, may charm thy glades to day—
Though dear Ionic music murmur not
Adown the vale—its echo all forgot!
Yet smile, beloved land! for soon, around,
Thy silent earth shall utter forth a sound,
As whilom—and, its pleasant groves among,
The Grecian voice shall breathe the Grecian song,
While the exilëd muse shall 'habit still
The happy haunts of her Parnassian hill.
Till then, behold the cold dumb sepulchre—
The ruin'd column—ocean, earth, and air,
Man, and his wrongs—thou hast Tyrtæus there! (*o*)

And pardon, if across the heaving main,
Sound the far melody of minstrel strain,
In wild and fitful gust from England's shore,
For *his* immortal sake, who never more

Shall tread with living foot, and spirit free,
Her fields, or breathe her passionate poetry—
The pilgrim bard, who lived, and died for thee,
Oh land of Memory ! loving thee no less
Than parent—with the filial tenderness,
And holy ardour of the Argive son,
Straining each nerve to bear thy chariot on—
Till when its wheels the place of glory swept,
He laid him down before the shrine—and slept.(*p*)

So be it ! at his cold unconscious bier,
We fondly sate, and dropp'd the natural tear—
Yet wept not wisely, for he sank to rest
On the dear earth his waking thoughts loved best,
And gently life's last pulses stole away !
No Moschus sang a requiem o'er his clay, (*q*)
But Greece was sad ! and breathed above, below,
The warrior's sigh, the silence, and the woe !

And is this all? Is this the little sum
For which we toil—to which our glories come?
Doth History bend her mouldering pages o'er,
And Science stretch her bulwark from the shore,
And Sages search the mystic paths of Thought,
And Poets charm with lays that Genius taught—
For this? to labour through their little day,
To weep an hour, then want the tear they pay—
To ask the urn, their death and life to tell,
When the dull dust would give that tale as well!

Man! hast thou seen the gallant vessel sweep,
Borrowing her moonlight from the jealous deep,
And gliding with mute foot, and silver wing,
Over the waters like a soul-mov'd thing?
Man, hast thou gazed on this—then look'd again,
And seen no speck on all that desolate main,

And heard no sound,—except the gurgling cry,
The winds half stifled in their mockery?

Woe unto thee! for, thus, thy course is run,
And, in the fulness of thy noon-day sun,
The darkness cometh—yea! thou walk'st abroad
In glory, Child of Mind, Creation's Lord—
And wisdom's music from thy lips hath gush'd!
Then comes the *Selah!* and the voice is hush'd, (*r*)
And the light past! we seek where thou hast been
In beauty—but thy beauty is not seen!
We breathe the air thou breath'dst, we tread the spot
Thy feet were wont to tread, but find thee not!
Beyond, sits Darkness with her haggard face,
Brooding fiend-like above thy burying-place—
Beneath, let wildest Fancy take her fill!
Shall we seek on? we shudder, and are still!

Yet woe not unto thee, thou child of Earth!
Though moonlight sleep on thy deserted hearth,
We will not cry 'Alas!' above thy clay!
It was, perchance, thy joyous pride to stray
On Mind's lone shore, and linger by the way:
But now thy pilgrim's staff is laid aside,
And on thou journeyest o'er the sullen tide,
To bless thy wearied sight, and glad thine heart
With all that Mind's serener skies impart;
Where Wisdom suns the day no shades destroy,
And Learning ends in Truth, as hope in joy:
While *we* stand mournful on the desert beach,
And wait, and wish, thy distant bark, to reach,
And weep to watch it passing from our sight,
And sound the gun's salute, and sigh our last 'good night!'

And oh! while thus the spirit glides away,—
Give to the world its memory with its clay!
Some page our country's grateful eyes may scan;
Some useful truth to bless surviving man;
Some name to honest bosoms justly dear;
Some grave t' exalt the thought, and claim the tear;
So when the pilgrim Sun is travelling o'er
The last blue hill, to gild a distant shore,
He leaves a freshness in the evening scene,
That tells Creation where his steps have been!

NOTES TO BOOK I.

Note (*a*).

Or peeps at glory from some ancient's back.

"The reason which the learned Bentley gave his daughter for not himself becoming an original writer, instead of wasting his talents on the works of others, is probably the cause of many not attempting original composition. Bentley seemed embarrassed at her honest question, and remained for a considerable time thoughtful. At length he observed—Child, I am sensible I have not always turned my talents to the proper use for which they were given me; yet I have done something: but the wit and genius of the old authors beguiled me, and as I despaired of raising myself up to their standard upon fair ground, I thought the only chance I had of looking over their heads was to get upon their shoulders."—*Curiosities of Literature, Vol. I.*

NOTE (*b*).

The gentle Cowley of our native clime
Lisp'd his first accents in Aonian rhyme.

A volume of Cowley's poems was published in his fifteenth year; and contains "The Tragical History of Pyramus and Thispe," written in his tenth.

NOTE (*c*).

Alfieri's startling muse tuned not her strings,
And dumbly look'd 'unutterable things,'
Till when five lustrums o'er his head had past—

This Poet's great mind exhibited no precocity. His 'Cleopatra,' written at the age of twenty-five years, first discovered its author's dramatic genius to himself, and to the world.

NOTE (*d*).

See in that breathless crowd Olorus stand,
While one fair boy hangs listening on his hand—
The young Thucydides.

It is said that Thucydides, in early youth, was present at the Olympic games when Herodotus recited his History; and that a burst of tears spoke his admiration. "Take care of that boy!" observed the sage turning to Olorus, "he will one day make a great man!"

NOTE (*e*).

That hail 'th' eternal city' in their pride.

"Imperium sine fine dedi," says Virgil's Jupiter. How little did the writer of those four words dream of their surviving the Glory, whose eternity they were intended to predict! Horace too, in the most exulting of his odes, boldly proclaims that his fame will live as long as

"Capitolium
Scandet cum tacitâ virgine Pontifex."

Yes! his fame *will live!*—but where now is the Pontifex, and the silent vestal? where now is the Capitol? Such passages are, to my mind, pre-eminently more affecting than all the ruins in the world!

NOTE (*f*).

And ultra Mitford soar'd to libel Greece.

Mr. Mitford's acknowledged learning, and accuracy in detail, have a claim on our consideration, which we admit with readiness and pleasure; but prejudices, arising probably from early habits and associations, have deformed his work. He is evidently so afraid of taking the mob for the people, that he constantly takes the people for the mob —a perversion much in vogue among despots of Europe, in the nineteenth century. He considers the Athenian Democracy as he would a classical kind of Radicalism; and generously endows Philip of Macedon with a 'right divine,' not only over his own possessions, but over those of his neighbours. Mr. Mitford lets his readers look at facts: but, whether shortsighted as himself or not, he will not allow them to enjoy that privilege unless they make use of his political glasses; which, by the way, are No. 20, —"ne plus ultra!"

Note (*g*).

But lean on Reason, as your safest rule!
Let doubtful facts, with patient hand be led
To take their place on this Procrustian bed.

We shall find some clever and animated observations on this subject, in Voltaire's preface to his Charles XII. I should extract them, but the book is too well known for me to doubt their having come to the knowledge of most readers: and a new publication is perhaps the only place, in which we are not glad to meet an old acquaintance.

NOTE (*h*).

Enlighten'd Miller of our modern days!

Those who may think this praise excessive are referred to the Philosophy of Modern History, given to the world by Dr. Miller; and thence are requested to judge of the reality of the merit.

NOTE (*i*).

The whisper'd sound which stole on Descartes' ear,
Hallowing the sunny visions of his youth,
With that eternal mandate, "Search for Truth!"

"Descartes, when young, and in a country seclusion, his brain exhausted by meditation, and his imagination heated to excess, heard a voice in the air which called him to pursue the search of Truth: he never doubted the vision, and this dream, in the delirium of Genius, charmed him even in his after studies."—*D'Israeli's Literary Character.*

NOTE (*j*).

He died the glorious! who, with soaring sight,
Sought some new world to plant his foot of might.

Archimedes wrote to Hiero, that, if he had another

world to stand on, he could move this by the power of his machinery. When Cicero stumbled on his grave, he found it, "Septum undique et vestitum vepribus et dumetis." What a homily!

Note (*k*).

So hard to bear with unobstructed sight,
Th' excess of darkness, or th' extreme of light.

Gray ingeniously asks, "Must I plunge into metaphysics?" (he might in some cases have said history)—"Alas! I cannot see in the dark; Nature has not furnished me with the optics of a cat. Must I pore upon mathematics? Alas! I cannot see in too much light; I am no eagle."

Note (*l*).

So Buffon erred—amidst his chilling dream
The judgment grew material as the theme.

Buffon was a materialist upon principle, though a Catholic by observance. Upon reading a poem on the immortality of the soul, he exclaimed—"Religion would be a noble present if this were true."

NOTE (*m*).

Sternly they strove—th' unequal race was run—

Leibnitz attacked with violence Sir Isaac Newton's opinion, that the seeds of mortality would be developed in the fabric of the universe if unrenewed by its divine Maker. Such an opinion he considered 'impious;' and, in opposition to it, maintained, that as Creation proceeded from the hand of Perfection, it is perfect—and as perfect, immutable.

NOTE (*n*).

Devoted Southey! if thou had'st not tried.

Few are ready to bear a more respectful tribute to Dr. Southey's poetical talents than the writer of this Work, who however begs to be allowed to admire his genius, without extending that admiration either to his politics or Hexameters.

NOTE (*o*).

Dwell not on parts, for parts contract the mind.

Lord Bacon thus expresses himself—"Sciences distinguished have a dependance upon universal knowledge, to be augmented, and rectified by the superior light thereof; as well as the parts and members of a science have upon the maxims of the same science, and the mutual light and consent which one part receiveth of another."—*Interpretatio Naturæ.*

NOTE (*p*).

For too much learning maketh no man mad.

Perhaps, after all, the great danger of knowing is in not knowing enough; and certainly "il pie fermo" is not "il piu basso." "It is true," says Lord Bacon, "that a little philosophy inclineth men's minds to atheism, but depth in philosophy bringeth their minds about to religion." This is an acute observation, and if generalized will be found equally so. The errors attending Intellectual Elevation I have alluded to and allowed; but that elevation is only comparative. "Alps on Alps arise!" and the *ars longa vita brevis* prevents our attaining the topmost height. In our progress towards it then is our risk—lest we rejoice to have gone a yard, without remembering we have a mile to go. Like the princess, in the pretty Arabian tale, who was ascending the mountain in search of her talking bird and golden water, if during the ascent we turn back to gaze, we are transformed into black stones—capable of impeding others, though not of advancing ourselves.

NOTE (*q*).

The sage how learned, and the man how meek!

The character of Sir Isaac Newton forms a sublime comment on the foregoing note. "I don't know," said that greatest and humblest of men, "what I may seem to the world; but as to myself, I seem to have been only like a boy playing on the sea-shore, and diverting myself in now and then finding a smoother pebble, or a prettier shell than ordinary, whilst the great ocean of Truth lay all undiscovered before me." — We find the anecdote in Spence.

NOTES TO BOOK II.

NOTE (*a*).

Ev'n Cato, had he own'd the senate's will,
And wash'd his toga—had been Cato still!

Plutarch relates that Cato Uticensis was thought to disgrace the Prætorship by the meanness of his dress. To couple 'disgrace' with the name of Cato revolts the soul; and yet who would call his "exigua toga" a *proof* of the loftiness of his virtue, or think him less a patriot if he had kept on his shoes?

NOTE (*b*).

"All is idea, and nothing real springs
But God and Reason!" (*not the right of kings?*)

An obvious question. Pyrrho the Elean, founder of the Ideal Philosophy, on the near approach of carts and carriages, did not think it worth while to turn aside, or change his posture. Dr. Berkeley, with less consistency, but more prudence, found time (and conscience) to write three sermons in vindication of passive obedience.

NOTE (*c*).

"*While (coldly studious!) thine ingenious scroll*
Endows the mimic statue with a soul,
Compos'd of sense."

It is the object of Condillac's work, 'Sur la Sensation,' to prove 'que la reflexion n'est dans son principe que la sensation meme,' and that our ideas are only sensation transformed. His statue is very cleverly put together, but is a *statue* after all.

NOTE (*d*).

What triumph hath the 'Art of Thinking' there?

"L'Art de penser"—title to one of Condillac's works.

NOTE (*e*).

To judge is your's—then why submissive call,
'The master said so?'

An 'argumentum ad verecundiam' used by the Pythagoreans. I so much admire a passage in Plato's Phædo, illustrative of these lines, that the reader must forgive my referring to it. Cebes supports with animation an opinion in opposition to Socrates, who, turning a gratified countenance ("ἡσθῆναι τε μοι ἔδοξε," says the narrator) to his other disciples, benignly observes—'Cebes always looks into principles; neither will he admit, without examination, the sentiments of any man.'

We find in Dr. Reid the following striking precept—"Let us, as becomes philosophers, lay aside authority."

NOTE (*f*).

If human faults to Plato's page belong,
Not ev'n with Plato willingly go wrong.

Cicero's assertion, "errare mehercule malo cum Platone quam cum istis vera sentire," is more boldly said than singularly thought. How many are there, among the canaille of readers, prepared to praise an inferior volume, with the Waverley magic on its *title-page;* to commend a commonplace by Rogers, or a far-fetched allusion by Moore. Even among the more critical of us, have the names of Scott, and Moore, and Rogers, no secret influence? Do we not so devoutly admire the noisy slippered Venus, that at length we begin to reverence, abstractedly, the noisy slippers? This is so, and I will not quarrel with it; since to forget the trifling faults of a great writer, is the gratitude we owe to his perfections. But what, in subjects of taste and sentiment, may be tolerated as pardonable enthusiasm, must in grave discussion, be condemned as unpardonable weakness. If therefore we judge Cicero only by the above-cited passage, we shall pronounce him to be a good Platonist, (in one sense of the word) but a very bad philosopher. It is not with him, 'Amicus Plato sed magis amica veritas:' he loves truth less than he loves Plato.

NOTE (*g*).

Or Memnon's statue singing 'neath the sun.

The statue of Memnon, the Ethiopian king, was said to utter musical sounds at the rising of the sun. Strabo witnessed this singular phenomenon, but could only explain it by conjecture.

NOTE (*h*).

But, ah! our Muse of Britain standing near,
Hath dimm'd my tablet with a pensive tear!

It is a practice too common, but manifestly unjust, to visit on the memory of distinguished authors their individual failings. I wish therefore to state expressly, that the Muse of Britain is not here supposed to animadvert on

Lord Bacon's character as a statesman, with which she has nothing to do in this place. It is with regard to his writings that I cannot avoid expressing a regret, and I do so reverentially, that pages so glorious should be polluted by passages so servile. "As men, we share his fame"—as Englishmen, we feel his degradation. If indeed the 'Novum organum,' and 'Advancement of Learning,' kindled our souls into a less proud consciousness of intellectual dignity, we might better brook hearing a king called 'a mortal god upon earth,' and James the First compared to Solomon. But Lord Bacon first teaches us how high Philosophy can soar, and then how low a philosopher can stoop.

Note (*i*).

And strikes Pierian chords—when Irving speaks!

There is a pleasure in being benefitted by the labours of Genius: there is a pride in possessing powers capable of benefitting. The pride Mr. Irving may justly feel; and which of his readers, or hearers, cannot boast the pleasure? It gratifies me to be enabled to express in this place my admiration of his talents, and my respect for their direction.

NOTE (*j*).

Ungrateful Plato! o'er thy cradled rest
The Muse hath hung, and all her love exprest.

Plato wrote poetry in his youth; and when indeed did not Plato write poetry? Longinus numbers him among the imitators of Homer—Πάντων δὲ τούτων μάλιστα ὁ Πλάτων ἀπὸ τοῦ Ὁμηρικοῦ ἐκείνου νάματος εἰς αὑτὸν μυρίας ὅσας παρατρόπας ἀποχετευσάμενος.

NOTE (*k*).

And as fair Eve, in Eden newly placed,
Gaz'd on her form, in limpid waters traced—

The reader will here perceive an allusion to that beautiful passage in Paradise Lost, book the fourth, where Eve describes to Adam her emotions on first beholding her own reflection in "the clear smooth lake"—

"A shape within the watery gleam appeared,
Bending to look on me—I started back—
It started back," &c.

NOTE (*l*).

The artist lingers in the moon-lit glade,
And light and shade, with him, are—light and shade.

"Quam multa vident Pictores in umbris et eminentia

quæ nos non videmus," is the motto to Mr. Price's admirable essay on the Picturesque. Dugald Stewart proposes its reversion—"Quam multa videmus nos quæ Pictores non vident," which if it be as true as ingenious, will go a great way in assisting my position.

Note (*m*).

——— to trace
Nature's ideal form in Nature's place.

Lord Bacon says of Poetry, that "it was ever thought to have some participation of divineness, because it doth raise and erect the mind, by submitting the shews of things to the desires of the mind; whereas Reason doth buckle and bow the mind unto the nature of things."—*Advancement of Learning, Book* 2.

Note (*n*).

Wherein Conception only dies in state,
As Draco smother'd by the garments' weight.

The Athenian People being accustomed to testify their approbation by the casting of their garments on the approved individual, Draco was honourably smothered through excess of popularity.

NOTE (*o*).

————behold the cold, dumb sepulchre,
The ruined column—ocean, earth and air,
Man and his wrongs!—thou hast Tyrtæus there!

The inspiriting effect of the productions of this Greek Poet, during the war between the Lacedæmonians and Messenians, is well known.

NOTE (*p*).

He laid him down before the shrine—and slept!

Herodotus relates of Cleobis and Bito, Argive brothers, that on a festival of Juno they themselves, in default of oxen, drew the chariot of the priestess, their mother, forty-five stadia to the temple. Amidst the shouts of an admiring multitude, their grateful parent asked of the gods the best boon mortals could receive, wherewith to reward the piety of her sons. The young men fell asleep within the temple, and woke no more.

NOTE (*q*).

No Moschus sang a requiem o'er his clay!

That exquisite effusion of Moschus over the grave of Bion, his "vatis amici"—his brother in poetry and love—will occur to the reader's recollection.

Note (*r*).

Then comes the Selah—*and the voice is hush'd!*

Respecting this Hebrew word, which is found "seventy times in the Psalms, and three times in Habakkuk," Calmet observes—"One conjecture is, that it means the end or a pause, and that the ancient musicians put it occasionally in the margin of their psalters, to shew where a musical pause was to be made, and where the tune ended."

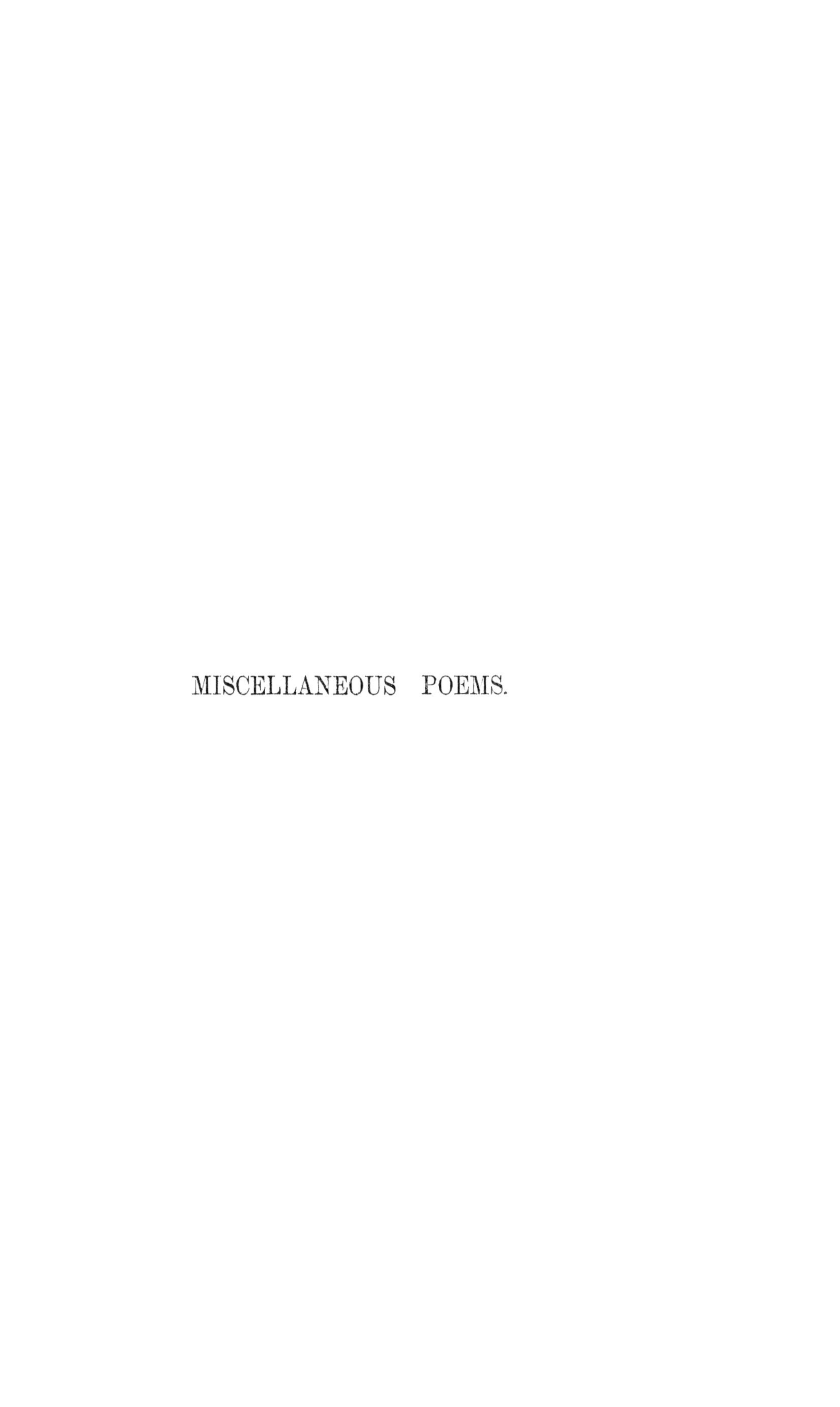

MISCELLANEOUS POEMS.

TO MY FATHER ON HIS BIRTH-DAY.

"Causa fuit Pater his."—Hor.

Amidst the days of pleasant mirth,
That throw their halo round our earth;
Amidst the tender thoughts that rise
To call bright tears to happy eyes;
Amidst the silken words that move
To syllable the names we love;
There glides no day of gentle bliss,
More soothing to the heart than *this!*
No thoughts of fondness e'er appear
More fond, than those I write of here!
No name can e'er on tablet shine,
My father! more belov'd than *thine!*

'Tis sweet, adown the shady past,
A lingering look of love to cast—
Back th' enchanted world to call,
That beamed around us first of all;
And walk with Memory fondly o'er
The paths, where Hope had been before—
Sweet to receive the sylphic sound
That breathes in tenderness around,
Repeating to the listening ear
The names that made our childhood dear—
For parted Joy, like Echo, kind,
Will leave her dulcet voice behind,
To tell, amidst the magic air,
How oft she smiled and lingered there.
Oh! let the deep Aonian shell
Breathe tuneful numbers, clear and well,
While the glad Hours, in fair array,
Lead on this buxom Holiday;

And Time, as on his way he springs,
Hates the last bard who gave him wings;
For 'neath thy gentleness of praise,
My Father! rose my early lays!
And when the lyre was scarce awake,
I lov'd its strings for *thy* lov'd sake;
Woo'd the kind Muses—but the while
Thought only how to win thy smile—
My proudest fame—my dearest pride—
More dear than all the world beside!
And now, perchance, I seek the tone
For magic that is more its own;
But still my Father's looks remain
The best Mæcenas of my strain;
My gentlest joy, upon his brow
To read the smile, that meets me now—
To hear him, in his kindness, say
The words,—perchance he'll speak to-day!

SPENSERIAN STANZAS

ON A BOY OF THREE YEARS OLD.

CHILD of the sunny lockes and beautifull brow!
In thoughtfull tendernesse I gaze on thee—
Upon thy daintie cheek Expression's glow
Daunceth in tyme to thine heart's melodie;
Ne mortall wight mote lovelier urchin see!
Nathlesse it teens this pensive brest of mine
To think—belive the innocent revelrie
Shall be eclipsed in those soft blue eyne—
Whenso the howre of youth no more for thee shall shine.

Ah me! eftsoons thy childhood's pleasaunt dais
Shall fly away, and be a whilome thing!

And sweetest mearimake, and birthday lais
Be reck'd not of, except when memories bring
Feres to their embers with awaking wing,
To make past love rejoyce thy tender sprite,
Albeit the toyles of daunger thee enring!
Child of the wavy lockes, and brow of light—
Then be thy conscience pure, as *now* thy face is bright.

VERSES TO MY BROTHER.

"For we were nurs'd upon the self-same hill."—LYCIDAS.

I WILL write down thy name, and when 'tis writ,
Will turn me from the hum that mortals keep
In the wide world without, and gaze on it!
It telleth of the past—calling from sleep
Such dear, yet mournful thoughts, as make us smile,
and weep.

Belov'd and best! what thousand feelings start,
As o'er the paper's course my fingers move—
My Brother! dearest, kindest as thou art!
How can these lips my heart's affection prove?
I could not speak the words, if words could speak
my love.

Together have we past our infant hours,
Together sported Childhood's spring away,
Together cull'd young Hope's fast budding flowers,
To wreathe the forehead of each coming day!
Yes! for the present's sun makes e'en the future gay.

And when the laughing mood was nearly o'er,
Together, many a minute did we wile
On Horace' page, or Maro's sweeter lore;
While one young critic, on the classic style,
Would sagely try to frown, and make the other smile.

But now alone thou con'st the ancient tome—
And sometimes thy dear studies, it may be,
Are cross'd by dearer dreams of me and home!
Alone I muse on Homer—thoughts are free—
And if mine often stray, they go in search of thee!

I may not praise thee *here*—I will not bless!
Yet all thy goodness doth my memory bear,
Cherish'd by more than Friendship's tenderness—
And, in the silence of my evening prayer,
Thou shalt not be forgot—thy dear name shall be
there!

STANZAS ON THE DEATH OF LORD BYRON.

" ———λέγε πᾶσιν ἀπώλετο."—BION.

" —I am not now
That which I have been."—CHILDE HAROLD.

HE *was*, and *is* not! Græcia's trembling shore,
Sighing through all her palmy groves, shall tell
That Harold's pilgrimage at last is o'er—
Mute the impassioned tongue, and tuneful shell,
That erst was wont in noblest strains to swell—
Hush'd the proud shouts that rode Ægæa's wave!
For lo! the great Deliv'rer breathes farewell!
Gives to the world his mem'ry and a grave—
Expiring in the land he only lived to save!

Mourn, Hellas, mourn! and o'er thy widow'd brow,
For aye, the cypress wreath of sorrow twine;
And in thy new-form'd beauty, desolate, throw
The fresh-cull'd flowers on *his* sepulchral shrine.
Yes! let that heart whose fervour was all thine,
In consecrated urn lamented be!
That generous heart where genius thrill'd divine,
Hath spent its last most glorious throb for thee—
Then sank amid the storm that made thy children free!

Britannia's Poet! Græcia's hero, sleeps!
And Freedom, bending o'er the breathless clay,
Lifts up her voice, and in her anguish weeps!
For *us*, a night hath clouded o'er our day,
And hush'd the lips that breath'd our fairest lay.

Alas! and must the British lyre resound
A requiem, while the spirit wings away
Of him who on its strings such music found,
And taught its startling chords to give so sweet a
sound!

The theme grows sadder—but my soul shall find
A language in these tears! No more—no more!
Soon, 'midst the shriekings of the tossing wind,
The 'dark blue depths' he sang of, shall have bore
Our *all* of Byron to his native shore!
His grave is thick with voices—to the ear
Murm'ring an awful tale of greatness o'er;
But Memory strives with Death, and lingering near,
Shall consecrate the dust of Harold's lonely bier!

MEMORY.

My Fancy's steps have often strayed
To some fair vale the hills have made;
Where sparkling waters travel o'er,
And hold a mirror to the shore;
Winding with murmurings in and out,
To find the flowers which grow about.
And there, perchance, in childhood bold,
Some little elf, four summers old,
Adown the vales may chance to run,
To hunt his shadow in the sun!
But when the waters meet his eyes,
He starts and stops with glad surprise,

And shouts, with merry voice, to view
The banks of green, the skies of blue,
Th' inverted flocks that bleating go,
Lilies, and trees of apple blow,
Seeming so beautiful below!
He peeps above—he glances round,
And then looks down, and thinks he's found
Reposing in the stream, to woo one,
A world ev'n lovelier than the true one.

Thus, with visions gay and light,
Hath Fancy lov'd my page to dight;
Yet Thought hath, through a vista, seen
Something less frivolous I ween:
Then, while my chatting pen runs on,
I'll tell you what she dreamt upon.

Memory's the streamlet of the scene,
Which sweeps the hills of life between;
And, when our walking hour is past,
Upon its shore we rest at last;
And love to view the waters fair,
And see lost joys depictured there.

My ——, when thy feet are led
To press those banks we all must tread—
May Virtue's smile, and Learning's praise,
Adorn the waters to thy gaze;
And, o'er their lucid course, be lent
The sunshine of a life well spent!
Then, if a thought should glad thy breast
Of those who loved thee first and best,
My name, perchance, may haunt the spot,
Not quite unprized—nor all forgot.

TO ———.

Mine is a wayward lay;
And, if its echoing rhymes I try to string,
Proveth a truant thing,
Whenso some names I love, send it away!

For then, eyes swimming o'er,
And claspëd hands, and smiles in fondness meant,
Are much more eloquent—
So it had fain begone, and speak no more!

Yet shall it come again,
Ah, friend belov'd! if so thy wishes be,
And, with wild melody,
I will, upon thine ear, cadence my strain—

Cadence my simple line,
Unfashion'd by the cunning hand of Art,
But coming from my heart,
To tell the message of its love to thine!

As ocean shells, when taken
From Ocean's bed, will faithfully repeat
Her ancient music sweet—
Ev'n so these words, true to my heart, shall waken!

Oh! while our bark is seen,
Our little bark of kindly, social love,
Down life's clear stream to move
Toward the summer shores, where all is green—

So long thy name shall bring,
Echoes of joy unto the grateful gales,
And thousand tender tales,
To freshen the fond hearts that round thee cling!

  Hast thou not look'd upon
The flowerets of the field in lowly dress?
  Blame not my simpleness—
Think only of my love!—my song is gone.

STANZAS

Occasioned by a passage in Mr. Emerson's Journal, which states, that on the mention of Lord Byron's name, Captain Demetrius, an old Roumeliot, burst into tears.

NAME not his name, or look afar—
For when my spirit hears
That name, its strength is turned to woe—
My voice is turned to tears.

Name me the host and battle-storm,
Mine own good sword shall stem ;
Name me the foeman and the block,
I have a smile for *them !*

But name *him* not, or cease to mark
This brow where passions sweep—
Behold, a warrior is a man,
And as a man may weep !

I could not scorn my Country's foes,
  Did not these tears descend—
I could not love my Country's fame,
  And not my Country's Friend.

Deem not his memory e'er can be
  Upon our spirits dim—
Name us the generous and the free,
  And we must think of *him!*

For his voice resounded through our land
  Like the voice of liberty,
As when the war-trump of the wind,
  Upstirs our dark blue sea.

His arm was in the foremost rank,
  Where embattled thousands roll—
His name was in the love of Greece,
  And his spell was on her soul!

But the arm that wielded her good sword,
The brow that wore the wreath,
The lips that breathed the deathless thoughts—
They went asleep in death.

Ye left his HEART, when ye took away
The dust in funeral state;
And we dumbly placed in a little urn,
That home of all things great.

The banner streamed—the war-shout rose—
Our heroes played their part;
But not a pulse would throb or burn—
Oh! could it be *his* heart!

I will not think—'tis worse than vain
Upon such thoughts to keep;
Then, Briton, name me not his name—
I cannot choose but weep!

THE PAST.

THERE is a silence upon the Ocean,
Albeit it swells with a feverish motion ;
Like to the battle-camp's fearful calm,
While the banners are spread, and the warriors arm.

The winds beat not their drum to the waves,
But sullenly moan in the distant caves ;
Talking over, before they rise,
Some of their dark conspiracies.

And so it is in this life of ours,
A calm may be on the present hours,
But the calmest hour of festive glee
May turn the mother of woe to thee.

G 3

I will betake me to the Past,
And she shall make my love at last;
I will find my home in her tarrying-place—
I will gaze all day on her deathly face!

Her form, though awful, is fair to view;
The clasp of her hand, though cold, is true;
Her shadowy brow hath no changefulness,
And her numbered smiles can grow no less!

Her voice is like a pleasant song,
Which we have not heard for very long,
And which a joy on our souls will cast,
Though we know not where we heard it last.

She shall walk with me, away, away,
Where'er the mighty have left their clay;
She shall speak to me in places lone,
With a low and holy tone.

Ay ! when I have lit my lamp at night,
She will be present with my sprite ;
And I will say, whate'er it be,
Every word she telleth me !

THE PRAYER.

Methought that I did stand upon a tomb—
And all was silent as the dust beneath,
While feverish thoughts upon my soul would come,
Losing my words in tears: I thought of death;
And prayed that when my lips gave out the breath,
The friends I loved like life might stay behind:
So, for a little while, my name might eath
Be something dear,—spoken with voices kind,
Heard with remembering looks, from eyes which
tears would blind!

I prayed that I might sink unto my rest,
(O foolish, selfish prayer!) before them all;
So I might look my last on those loved best—

So never would my voice repining call,
And never would my tears impassioned fall
On one familiar face turning to clay!
So would my tune of life be musical,
Albeit abrupt—like airs the Spaniards play,
Which in the sweetest part, break off, and die away.

Methought I looked around! the scene was rife
With little vales, green banks, and waters heaving;
And every living thing did joy in life,
And every thing of beauty did seem living—
Oh, then, life's pulse was at my heart reviving;
And then I knew that it was good to bear
Dispensëd woe, that by the spirit's grieving,
It might be weanëd from a world so fair!—
Thus with submissive words mine heart did close its prayer.

ON A PICTURE OF RIEGO'S WIDOW,

PLACED IN THE EXHIBITION.

DAUGHTER of Spain! a passer by
  May mark the cheek serenely pale—
The dark eyes which dream silently,
  And the calm lip which gives no wail!

Calm! it bears not a deeper trace
  Of feelings it disdained to show;
We look upon the Widow's face,
  And only read the Patriot's woe!

No word, no look, no sigh of thine,
  Would make *his* glory seem more dim;
Thou would'st not give to vulgar eyne
  The sacred tear which fell for HIM.

Thou would'st not hold to the world's view
  Thy ruined joys, thy broken heart—
The jeering world—it only knew
  Of all thine anguish—that thou WERT !

While o'er *his* grave thy steps would go
  With a firm tread,—stilling thy love,—
As if the dust would blush below
  To feel one faltering foot above.

For Spain, *he* dared the noble strife—
  For Spain, he gave his latest breath ;
And he who lived the Patriot's life,
  Was dragged to die the traitor's death !

And the shout of thousands swept around,
  As he stood the traitor's block beside ;
But his dying lips gave a free sound—
  Let the foe weep !—THY brow had *pride !*

Yet haply in the midnight air,
When none might part thy God and thee,
The lengthened sob, the passionate prayer,
Have spoken thy soul's agony!

But silent else, thou past away—
The plaint unbreath'd, the anguish hid—
More voiceless than the echoing clay
Which idly knocked thy coffin's lid.

Peace be to thee! while Britons seek
This place, if British souls they bear,
'Twill start the crimson in the cheek
To see Riego's widow THERE!

SONG.

WEEP, as if you thought of laughter!
Smile, as tears were coming after!
Marry your pleasures to your woes;
And think life's green well worth its rose!

No sorrow will your heart betide,
Without a comfort by its side;
The sun may sleep in his sea-bed,
But you have starlight overhead.

Trust not to Joy! the rose of June,
When opened wide, will wither soon;
Italian days without twilight,
Will turn them suddenly to night.

Joy, most changeful of all things,
Flits away on rainbow wings;
And when they look the gayest, know,
It is that they are spread to go!

THE DREAM.

A FRAGMENT.

I HAD a dream!—my spirit was unbound
From the dark iron of its dungeon, clay,
And rode the steeds of Time;—my thoughts had
sound,
And spoke without a word,—I went away
Among the buried ages, and did lay
The pulses of my heart beneath the touch
Of the rude minstrel Time, that he should play
Thereon, a melody which might seem such
As musing spirits love—mournful, but not too much!

I had a dream—and there mine eyes did see
The shadows of past deeds like present things—
The sepulchres of Greece and Hespery,

Ægyptus, and old landes, gave up their kings,
Their prophets, saints, and minstrels, whose lute-
strings
Keep a long echo—yea, the dead, white bones,
Did stand up by the house whereto Death clings,
And dressed themselves in life, speaking of thrones,
And fame, and power, and beauty, in familiar tones!

I went back further still, for I beheld
What time the earth was one fair Paradise—
And over such bright meads the waters welled,
I wot the rainbow was content to rise
Upon the earth, when absent from the skies!
And there were tall trees that I never knew,
Whereon sate nameless birds in merry guise,
Folding their radiant wings, as the flowers do,
When summer nights send sleep down with the dew.

* * * * *

Anon there came a change—a terrible motion,
That made all living things grow pale and shake!
The dark Heavens bowed themselves unto the
ocean,
Like a strong man in strife—Ocean did take
His flight across the mountains; and the lake
Was lashed into a sea where the winds ride—
Earth was no more, for in her merrymake
She had forgot her God—Sin claimed his bride,
And with his vampire breath sucked out her life's
fair tide!

Life went back to her nostrils, and she raised
Her spirit from the waters once again—
The lovely sights, on which I erst had gazed,
Were *not*—though she was beautiful as when
The Grecian called her "Beauty"—sinful men

Walked i' the track of the waters, and felt bold—
Yea, they looked up to Heaven in calm disdain,
As if no eye had seen its vault unfold
Darkness, and fear, and death!—as if a tale were
told!

And ages fled away within my dream;
And still Sin made the heart his dwelling-place,
Eclipsing Heaven from men; but it would seem
That two or three dared commune face to face,
And speak of the soul's life, of hope, and grace—
Anon there rose such sounds as angels breathe—
For a God came to die, bringing down peace—
"Pan *was not*;" and the darkness that did wreathe
The earth, past from the soul—Life came by death!

* * * * *

RIGA'S LAST SONG.

I HAVE looked my last on my native land,
And over these strings I throw my hand,
To say in the death-hour's minstrelsy,
Hellas, my country! farewell to thee!

I have looked my last on my native shore;
I shall tread my country's plains no more;
But my last thought is of her fame;
But my last breath speaketh her name!

And though these lips shall soon be still,
They may now obey the spirit's will;
Though the dust be fettered, the spirit is free—
Hellas, my country! farewell to thee!

I go to death—but I leave behind
The stirrings of Freedom's mighty mind;
Her voice shall arise from plain to sky,
Her steps shall tread where my ashes lie!

I looked on the mountains of proud Souli,
And the mountains they seemed to look on me;
I spoke my thought on Marathon's plain,
And Marathon seemed to speak again!

And as I journeyed on my way,
I saw an infant group at play;
One shouted aloud in his childish glee,
And showed me the heights of Thermopylæ!

I gazed on peasants hurrying by,—
The dark Greek pride crouched in their eye;
So I swear in my death-hour's minstrelsy,
Hellas, my country! thou *shalt* be free!

No more!—I dash my lyre on the ground—
I tear its strings from their home of sound—
For the music of slaves shall never keep
Where the hand of a freeman was wont to sweep!

And I bend my brows above the block,
Silently waiting the swift death shock;
For these lips shall speak what becomes the free—
Or—Hellas, my country! farewell to thee!

He bowed his head with a Patriot's pride,
And his dead trunk fell the mute lyre beside!
The soul of each had past away—
Soundless the strings—breathless the clay!

THE VISION OF FAME.

Did ye ever sit on summer noon,
  Half musing and half asleep,
When ye smile in such a dreamy way,
  Ye know not if ye weep—

When the little flowers are thick beneath,
  And the welkin blue above;
When there is not a sound but the cattle's low,
  And the voice of the woodland dove?

A while ago and I dreamëd thus—
  I mused on ancient story,—
For the heart like a minstrel of old doth seem,
  It delighteth to sing of glory.

What time I saw before me stand,
  A bright and lofty One;
A golden lute was in her hand,
  And her brow drooped thereon.

But the brow that drooped was raisëd soon,
  Shewing its royal sheen—
It was, I guessed, no human brow,
  Though pleasant to human een.

And this brow of peerless majesty,
  With its whiteness did enshroud
Two eyes, that, darkly mystical,
  'Gan look up at a cloud.

Like to the hair of Berenice,
  Fetch'd from its house of light,
Was the hair which wreathed her shadowless form—
  And Fame the ladye hight!

But as she wended on to me,
  My heart's deep fear was chidden;
For she called up the sprite of Melody,
  Which in her lute lay hidden.

When ye speak to well-beloved ones,
  Your voice is tender and low :
The wires methought did love her touch—
  For they did answer so.

And her lips in such a quiet way
  Gave the chant soft and long,—
You might have thought she only breathed,
  And that her breath was song :—

  "When Death shrouds thy memory,
      Love is no shrine—
  The dear eyes that weep for thee,
      Soon sleep like thine !

The wail murmured over thee,
Fainteth away ;
And the heart which kept love for thee,
Turns into clay !

" But would'st thou remembered be,
Make me thy vow ;
This verse that flows gushingly,
Telleth thee how—
Linking thy hand in mine,
Listen to me,
So not a thought of thine
Dieth with thee—

" Rifle thy pulsing heart
Of the gift, love made ;
Bid thine eye's light depart ;
Let thy cheek fade !

Give me the slumber deep,
  Which night-long seems;
Give me the joys that creep
  Into thy dreams!

"Give me thy youthful years,
  Merriest that fly—
So the word, spoke in *tears,*
  Liveth for aye!
So thy sepulchral stone,
  Nations may raise—
What time thy soul hath known
  The *worth of praise!*"

She did not sing this chant to me,
  Though I was sitting by;
But I listened to it with chainëd breath,
  That had no power to sigh.

And ever as the chant went on,
  Its measure changed to wail;
And ever as the lips sang on,
  Her face did grow more pale.

Paler and paler—till anon
  A fear came o'er my soul;
For the flesh curled up from her bones,
  Like to a blasted scroll!

Ay! silently it dropped away,
  Before my wondering sight—
There was only a bleachëd skeleton,
  Where erst was ladye bright!

But still the vacant sockets gleamed
  With supernatural fires—
But still the boney hands did ring
  Against the shuddering wires!

Alas, alas! I wended home,
  With a sorrow and a shame—
Is Fame the rest of our poor hearts?
  Woe's me! for THIS is FAME!

MISCELLANEOUS POEMS.

[Published 1833.]

[The following pieces were published at the end of a volume entitled—

Prometheus Bound. Translated from the Greek of Æschylus, and Miscellaneous Poems, by the Translator, Author of "An Essay on Mind," with other Poems.

Τὸ πρὶν ἐὼν κάλλιστος—

Mimnermus.

Ἐγγύθεν αὐλητῆρος ἀείσομαι.—

Theognis.

London, Printed and Published by A. J. Valpy, M.A. Red Lion-court, Fleet-street. 1833.]

CONTENTS.

CONTENTS.

THE TEMPEST.

A FRAGMENT.

'Mors erat ante oculos."
LUCAN, lib. ix.

---

*   *   *   *

The forest made my home—the voiceful streams
My minstrel throng: the everlasting hills,—
Which marry with the firmament, and cry
Unto the brazen thunder, 'Come away,
Come from thy secret place, and try our strength,—'
Enwrapp'd me with their solemn arms. Here, light
Grew pale as darkness, scarëd by the shade
O' the forest Titans. Here, in piny state,
Reign'd Night, the Æthiopian queen, and crown'd

The charmëd brow of Solitude, her spouse.

* * * * * * * *
* * * * * * * *
* * * * * * * *

A sign was on creation. You beheld
All things encolour'd in a sulph'rous hue,
As day were sick with fear. The haggard clouds
O'erhung the utter lifelessness of air;
The top boughs of the forest all aghast,
Stared in the face of Heav'n; the deep-mouth'd wind,
That hath a voice to bay the armëd sea,
Fled with a low cry like a beaten hound;
And only that askance the shadows, flew
Some open-beakëd birds in wilderment,
Naught stirr'd abroad. All dumb did Nature seem,
In expectation of the coming storm.

It came in power. You soon might hear afar
The footsteps of the martial thunder sound

Over the mountain battlements ; the sky
Being deep-stain'd with hues fantastical,
Red like to blood, and yellow like to fire,
And black like plumes at funerals ; overhead
You might behold the lightning faintly gleam
Amid the clouds which thrill and gape aside,
And straight again shut up their solemn jaws,
As if to interpose between Heaven's wrath
And Earth's despair. Interposition brief!
Darkness is gathering out her mighty pall
Above us, and the pent-up rain is loosed,
Down trampling in its fierce delirium.

Was not my spirit gladden'd, as with wine,
To hear the iron rain, and view the mark
Of battle on the banner of the clouds?
Did I not hearken for the battle-cry,
And rush along the bowing woods to meet

The riding Tempest—skyey cataracts
Hissing around him with rebellion vain?
Yea! and I lifted up my glorying voice
In an 'All hail;' when, wildly resonant,
As brazen chariots rushing from the war,
As passion'd waters gushing from the rock,
As thousand crashëd woods, the thunder cried:
And at his cry the forest tops were shook
As by the woodman's axe; and far and near
Stagger'd the mountains with a mutter'd dread.

All hail unto the lightning! hurriedly
His lurid arms are glaring through the air,
Making the face of heav'n to show like hell!
Let him go breathe his sulphur stench about,
And, pale with death's own mission, lord the storm!
Again the gleam—the glare: I turn'd to hail
Death's mission: at my feet there lay the dead!

The dead—the dead lay there! I could not view
(For Night espoused the storm, and made all dark)
Its features, but the lightning in his course
Shiver'd above a white and corpse-like heap,
Stretch'd in the path, as if to show his prey,
And have a triumph ere he pass'd. Then I
Crouch'd down upon the ground, and groped about
Until I touch'd that thing of flesh, rain-drench'd,
And chill, and soft. Nathless, I did refrain
My soul from natural horror! I did lift
The heavy head, half-bedded in the clay,
Unto my knee; and pass'd my fingers o'er
The wet face, touching every lineament,
Until I found the brow; and chafed its chill,
To know if life yet linger'd in its pulse.
And while I was so busied, there did leap
From out the entrails of the firmament,
The lightning, who his white unblenching breath
Blew in the dead man's face, discov'ring it

As by a staring day- I knew that face—
His, who did hate me—his, whom I did hate!

I shrunk not—spake not--sprang not from the ground!
But felt my lips shake without cry or breath,
And mine heart wrestle in my breast to still
The tossing of its pulses; and a cold,
Instead of living blood, o'ercreep my brow.
Albeit such darkness brooded all around,
I had dread knowledge that the open eyes
Of that dead man were glaring up to mine,
With their unwinking, unexpressive stare;
And mine I could not shut nor turn away.
The man was my familiar. I had borne
Those eyes to scowl on me their living hate,
Better than I could bear their deadliness:
I had endured the curses of those lips,
Far better than their silence. Oh constrain'd
And awful silence!—awful peace of death!

There is an answer to all questioning,
That one word—*death.* Our bitterness can throw
No look upon the face of death, and live.
The burning thoughts that erst my soul illumed,
Were quench'd at once; as tapers in a pit
Wherein the vapour-witches weirdly reign
In charge of darkness. Farewell all the past!
It was out-blotted from my memory's eyes,
When clay's cold silence pleaded for its sin.

Farewell the elemental war! farewell
The clashing of the shielded clouds—the cry
Of scathëd echoes! I no longer knew
Silence from sound, but wander'd far away
Into the deep Eleusis of mine heart,
To learn its secret things. When armëd foes
Meet on one deck with impulse violent,
The vessel quakes thro' all her oaken ribs,
And shivers in the sea; so with mine heart:

For there had battled in her solitudes,
Contrary spirits; sympathy with power,
And stooping unto power;—the energy
And passiveness,—the thunder and the death!

Within me was a nameless thought: it closed
The Janus of my soul on echoing hinge,
And said 'Peace!' with a voice like War's. I bow'd,
And trembled at its voice: it gave a key,
Empower'd to open out all mysteries
Of soul and flesh; of man, who doth begin,
But endeth not; of life, and *after life.*

* * * * * * * *

Day came at last: her light show'd gray and sad,
As hatch'd by tempest, and could scarce prevail
Over the shaggy forest to imprint
Its outline on the sky—expressionless,
Almost sans shadow as sans radiance:
An idiocy of light. I waken'd from

My deep unslumb'ring dream, but utter'd naught.
My living I uncoupled from the dead,
And look'd out, 'mid the swart and sluggish air,
For place to make a grave. A mighty tree
Above me, his gigantic arms outstretch'd,
Poising the clouds. A thousand mutter'd spells
Of every ancient wind and thun'drous storm,
Had been off-shaken from his scathless bark.
He had heard distant years sweet concord yield,
And go to silence ; having firmly kept
Majestical companionship with Time.
Anon his strength wax'd proud : his tusky roots
Forced for themselves a path on every side,
Riving the earth ; and, in their savage scorn,
Casting it from them like a thing unclean,
Which might impede his naked clambering
Unto the heavens. Now blasted, peel'd, he stood,
By the gone night, whose lightning had come in
And rent him, even as it rent the man

Beneath his shade : and there the strong and weak
Communion join'd in deathly agony.

There, underneath, I lent my feverish strength,
To scoop a lodgment for the traveller's corse.
I gave it to the silence and the pit,
And strew'd the heavy earth on all : and then—
I—I, whose hands had form'd that silent house,—
I could not look thereon, but turn'd and wept !

* * * * * * * *

* * * * * * * *

Oh Death—oh crownëd Death—pale-steedëd Death !
Whose name doth make our respiration brief,
Muffling the spirit's drum ! Thou, whom men know
Alone by charnel-houses, and the dark
Sweeping of funeral feathers, and the scath
Of happy days,—love deem'd inviolate !
Thou of the shrouded face, which to have seen
Is to be very awful, like thyself !—

Thou, whom all flesh shall see!—thou, who dost call,
And there is none to answer!—thou, whose call
Changeth all beauty into what we fear,
Changeth all glory into what we tread,
Genius to silence, wrath to nothingness,
And love—not love!—thou hast no change for love!
Thou, who art Life's betroth'd, and bear'st her forth
To scare her with sad sights,—who hast thy joy
Where'er the peopled towns are dumb with plague,—
Where'er the battle and the vulture meet,—
Where'er the deep sea writhes like Laocoon
Beneath the serpent winds, and vessels split
On secret rocks, and men go gurgling down,
Down, down, to lose their shriekings in the depth
Oh universal thou! who comest aye
Among the minstrels, and their tongue is tied;—
Among the sophists, and their brain is still;—
Among the mourners, and their wail is done;—
Among the dancers, and their tinkling feet
No more make echoes on the tombing earth;—

Among the wassail rout, and all the lamps
Are quench'd; and wither'd the wine-pouring hands!

Mine heart is armëd not in panoply
Of the old Roman iron, nor assumes
The Stoic valour. 'Tis a human heart
And so confesses, with a human fear;—
That only for the hope the cross inspires,
That only for the MAN who died and lives,
'Twould crouch beneath thy sceptre's royalty,
With faintness of the pulse, and backward cling
To life. But knowing what I soothly know,
High-seeming Death, I dare thee! and have hope,
In God's good time, of showing to thy face
An unsuccumbing spirit, which sublime
May cast away the low anxieties
That wait upon the flesh—the reptile moods;
And enter that eternity to come,
Where live the dead, and only Death shall die.

A SEA-SIDE MEDITATION.

"Ut per aquas quæ nunc rerum simulacra videmus.
LUCRETIUS, lib. .

Go, travel 'mid the hills! The summer's hand
Hath shaken pleasant freshness o'er them all.
Go, travel 'mid the hills! There, tuneful streams
Are touching myriad stops, invisible;
And winds, and leaves, and birds, and your own thoughts,
(Not the least glad) in wordless chorus, crowd
Around the thymele* of Nature.

---

* The central point of the choral movements in the Greek theatre.

Go,
And travel onward. Soon shall leaf and bird,
Wind, stream, no longer sound. Thou shalt behold
Only the pathless sky, and houseless sward;
O'er which anon are spied innumerous sails
Of fisher vessels like the wings o' the hill,
And white as gulls above them, and as fast.—
But sink they—sink they out of sight. And now
The wind is springing upward in your face;
And, with its fresh-toned gushings, you may hear
Continuous sound which is not of the wind,
Nor of the thunder, nor o' the cataract's
Deep passion, nor o' the earthquake's wilder pulse;
But which rolls on in stern tranquillity,
As memories of evil o'er the soul;—
Boweth the bare broad Heav'n.—What view you?
sea—and sea!

The sea—the glorious sea! from side to side,

Swinging the grandeur of his foamy strength,
And undersweeping the horizon,—on—
On—with his life and voice inscrutable.
Pause : sit you down in silence ! I have read
Of that Athenian, who, when ocean raged,
Unchain'd the prison'd music of his lips,
By shouting to the billows, sound for sound.
I marvel how his mind would let his tongue
Affront thereby the ocean's solemness.
Are we not mute, or speak restrainedly,
When overhead the trampling tempests go,
Dashing their lightning from their hoofs ? and when
We stand beside the bier ? and when we see
The strong bow down to weep—and stray among
Places which dust or mind hath sanctified ?
Yea ! for such sights and acts do tear apart
The close and subtle clasping of a chain,
Form'd not of gold, but of corroded brass,
Whose links are furnish'd from the common mine

Of every day's event, and want, and wish ;
From work-times, diet-times, and sleeping-times :
And thence constructed, mean and heavy links
Within the pandemonic walls of sense,
Enchain our deathless part, constrain our strength,
And waste the goodly stature of our soul.

Howbeit, we love this bondage ; we do cleave
Unto the sordid and unholy thing,
Fearing the sudden wrench required to break
Those claspëd links. Behold ! all sights and sounds
In air, and sea, and earth, and under earth,
All flesh, all life, all ends, are mysteries ;
And all that is mysterious dreadful seems,
And all we cannot understand we fear.
Ourselves do scare ourselves : we hide our sight
In artificial nature from the true,
And throw sensation's veil associative
On God's creation, man's intelligence ;

Bowing our high imaginings to eat
Dust, like the serpent, once erect as they;
Binding conspicuous on our reason's brow
Phylacteries of shame; learning to feel
By rote, and act by rule, (man's rule, not God's!)
Until our words grow echoes, and our thoughts
A mechanism of spirit.

Can this last?

No! not for aye. We cannot subject aye
The heav'n-born spirit to the earth-born flesh.
Tame lions *will* scent blood, and appetite
Carnivorous glare from out their restless eyes.
Passions, emotions, sudden changes, throw
Our nature back upon us, till we burn.
What warm'd Cyrene's fount? As poets sing,
The *change* from light to dark, from dark to light.

All that doth force this nature back on us,
All that doth force the mind to view the mind,

Engend'reth what is named by men, *sublime.*
Thus when, our wonted valley left, we gain
The mountain's horrent brow, and mark from thence
The sweep of lands extending with the sky;
Or view the spanless plain; or turn our sight
Upon yon deep's immensity;—we breathe
As if our breath were marble: to and fro
Do reel our pulses, and our words are mute.
We cannot mete by parts, but grapple all:
We cannot measure with our eye, but soul;
And fear is on us. The extent unused,
Our spirit, sends, to spirit's element,
To seize upon abstractions: first on space,
The which *eternity in place,* I deem;
And then upon eternity; till thought
Hath form'd a mirror from their secret sense,
Wherein we view ourselves, and back recoil
At our own awful likeness; ne'ertheless,
Cling to that likeness with a wonder wild,

And while we tremble, glory—proud in fear.

So ends the prose of life : and so shall be
Unlock'd her poetry's magnific store.
And so, thou pathless and perpetual sea,
So, o'er thy deeps, I brooded and must brood,
Whether I view thee in thy dreadful peace,
Like a spent warrior hanging in the sun
His glittering arms, and meditating death ;
Or whether thy wild visage gath'reth shades,
What time thou marshall'st forth thy waves who hold
A covenant of storms, then roar and wind
Under the rocking rocks ; as martyrs lie
Wheel-bound ; and, dying, utter lofty words !
Whether the strength of day is young and high,
Or whether, weary of the watch, he sits
Pale on thy wave, and weeps himself to death ;—
In storm and calm, at morn and eventide,
Still have I stood beside thee, and out-thrown

My spirit onward on thine element,—
Beyond thine element,— to tremble low
Before those feet which trod thee as they trod
Earth,—to the holy, happy, peopled place,
Where there is no more sea. Yea, and my soul,
Having put on thy vast similitude,
Hath wildly moanëd at her proper depth,
Echoed her proper musings, veil'd in shade
Her secrets of decay, and exercised
An elemental strength, in casting up
Rare gems and things of death on fancy's shore,
Till Nature said, 'Enough.'
Who longest dreams,
Dreams not for ever; seeing day and night
And corporal feebleness divide his dreams,
And, on his elevate creations weigh
With hunger, cold, heat, darkness, weariness:
Else should we be like gods; else would the course
Of thought's free wheels, increased in speed and might,

By an eterne volution, oversweep
The heights of wisdom, and invade her depths:
So, knowing all things, should we have all power;
For is not Knowledge power? But mighty spells
Our operation sear; the Babel must,
Or ere it touch the sky, fall down to earth:
The web, half form'd, must tumble from our hands,
And, ere they can resume it, lie decay'd.
Mind struggles vainly from the flesh. E'en so,
Hell's angel (saith a scroll apocryphal)
Shall, when the latter days of earth have shrunk
Before the blast of God, affect his heav'n;
Lift his scarr'd brow, confirm his rebel heart,
Shoot his strong wings, and darken pole and pole,—
Till day be blotted into night; and shake
The fever'd clouds, as if a thousand storms
Throbb'd into life! Vain hope—vain strength—vain flight!
God's arm shall meet God's foe, and hurl him back!

A VISION OF LIFE AND DEATH.

MINE ears were deaf to melody,
  My lips were dumb to sound:
Where didst thou wander, oh my soul,
  When ear and tongue were bound?

'I wander'd by the stream of time,
  Made dark by human tears:
I threw my voice upon the waves,
  And *they* did throw me theirs.'

And how did sound the waves, my soul?
  And how did sound the waves?
'Hoarse, hoarse, and wild!—they ever dash'd
  'Gainst ruin'd thrones and graves.'

And what sight on the shore, my soul?
  And what sight on the shore?
'Twain beings sate there silently,
  And sit there evermore.'

Now tell me fast and true, my soul;
  Now tell me of those twain.
'One was yclothed in mourning vest,
  And one, in trappings vain.

'She, in the trappings vain, was fair,
  And eke fantastical:
A thousand colours dyed her garb;
  A blackness bound them all.

'In part her hair was gaily wreath'd,
  In part was wildly spread:
Her face did change its hue too fast,
  To say 'twas pale or red.

'And when she look'd on earth, I thought
She smiled for very glee:
But when she look'd to heav'n, I knew
That tears stood in her ee.

'She held a mirror, there to gaze:
It could no cheer bestow;
For while her beauty cast the shade,
Her breath did make it go.

'A harper's harp did lie by her,
Without the harper's hest;
A monarch's crown did lie by her,
Wherein an owl had nest:

'A warrior's sword did lie by her,
Grown rusty since the fight;
A poet's lamp did lie by her:—
Ah me!—where was its light?'

And what didst *thou* say, O, my soul,
Unto that mystic dame?
'I ask'd her of her tears, and eke
I ask'd her of her name.

'She said, she built a prince's throne:
She said, he ruled the grave;
And that the levelling worm ask'd not
If he were king or slave.

'She said, she form'd a godlike tongue,
Which lofty thoughts unsheathed;
Which roll'd its thunder round, and purged
The air the nations breathed.

'She said, that tongue, all eloquent,
With silent dust did mate;
Whereon false friends betray'd long faith,
And foes outspat their hate.

She said, she warm'd a student's heart,
But heart and brow 'gan fade :
Alas, alas ! those Delphic trees
Do cast an upas shade !

'She said, she lighted happy hearths,
Whose mirth was all forgot :
She said, she tunëd marriage bells,
Which rang when love was *not.*

'She said, her name was Life ; and then
Out laugh'd and wept aloud,—
What time the other being strange
Lifted the veiling shroud.

'Yea ! lifted she the veiling shroud,
And breathed the icy breath ;
Whereat, with inward shuddering,
I knew *her* name was Death.

'Yea! lifted she her calm, calm brow,
  Her clear cold smile on me:
Whereat within my deepness, leap'd
  Mine immortality.

'She told me, it did move her smile,
  To witness how I sigh'd,
Because that what was fragile brake,
  And what was mortal died:

'As if that kings could grasp the earth,
  Who from its dust began;
As if that suns could shine at night,
  Or glory dwell with man.

'She told me, she had freed *his* soul,
  Who aye did freedom love;
Who now reck'd not, were worms below,
  Or ranker worms above!

'She said, the student's heart had beat
Against its prison dim;
Until she crush'd the bars of flesh,
And pour'd truth's light on him.

'She said, that they who left the hearth,
For aye in sunshine dwell;
She said, the funeral tolling brought
More joy than marriage bell!

'And as she spake, she spake less loud;
The stream resounded more:
Anon I nothing heard but waves
That wail'd along the shore.'

And what didst thou say, oh my soul,
Upon that mystic strife?
'I said, that Life was only Death,
That only Death was Life.'

EARTH.

How beautiful is earth! my starry thoughts
Look down on it from their unearthly sphere,
And sing symphonious—Beautiful is earth!
The lights and shadows of her myriad hills;
The branching greenness of her myriad woods;
Her sky-affecting rocks; her zoning sea;
Her rushing, gleaming cataracts; her streams
That race below, the wingèd clouds on high;
Her pleasantness of vale and meadow!—

Hush!
Meseemeth through the leafy trees to ring
A chime of bells to falling waters tuned;

Whereat comes heathen Zephyrus, out of breath
With running up the hills, and shakes his hair
From off his gleesome forehead, bold and glad
With keeping blythe Dan Phœbus company;—
And throws him on the grass, though half afraid;
First glancing round, lest tempests should be nigh;
And lays close to the ground his ruddy lips,
And shapes their beauty into sound, and calls
On all the petall'd flowers that sit beneath
In hiding-places from the rain and snow,
To loosen the hard soil, and leave their cold
Sad idlesse, and betake them up to him.
They straightway hear his voice—

A thought did come,
And press from out my soul the heathen dream.
Mine eyes were purgëd. Straightway did I bind
Round me the garment of my strength, and heard
Nature's death-shrieking—the hereafter cry,

When he o' the lion voice, the rainbow-crown'd,
Shall stand upon the mountains and the sea,
And swear by earth, by heaven's throne, and Him
Who sitteth on the throne, there shall be time
No more, no more! Then, veil'd Eternity
Shall straight unveil her awful countenance
Unto the reeling worlds, and take the place
Of seasons, years, and ages. Aye and aye
Shall be the time of day. The wrinkled heav'n
Shall yield her silent sun, made blind and white
With an exterminating light: the wind,
Unchainëd from the poles, nor having charge
Of cloud or ocean, with a sobbing wail
Shall rush among the stars, and swoon to death.
Yea, the shrunk earth, appearing livid pale
Beneath the red-tongued flame, shall shudder by
From out her ancient place, and leave—a void.
Yet haply by that void the saints redeem'd
May sometimes stray; when memory of sin

Ghost-like shall rise upon their holy souls;
And on their lips shall lie the name of earth
In paleness and in silentness; until
Each looking on his brother, face to face,
And bursting into sudden happy tears,
(The only tears undried) shall murmur—'Christ!'

THE PICTURE GALLERY AT PENSHURST.

THEY spoke unto me from the silent ground,
They look'd unto me from the pictured wall;
The echo of my footstep was a sound
Like to the echo of their own footfall,
What time their living feet were in the hall.
I breathed where they had breathed—and where
they brought
Their souls to moralize on glory's pall,
I walk'd with silence in a cloud of thought:
So, what they erst had learn'd, I mine own spirit
taught.

Ay ! with mine eyes of flesh, I did behold
The likeness of their flesh ! They, the great dead,
Stood still upon the canvass, while I told
The glorious memories to their ashes wed.
There, I beheld the Sidneys :—he, who bled
Freely for freedom's sake, bore gallantly
His soul upon his brow ;—he, whose lute said
Sweet music to the land, meseem'd to be
Dreaming with that pale face, of love and Arcadie.

Mine heart had shrinëd these. And therefore past
Where these, and such as these, in mine heart's pride,
Which deem'd death, glory's other name. At last
I stay'd my pilgrim feet, and paused beside
A picture,* which the shadows half did hide.
The form was a fair woman's form ; the brow
Brightly between the clustering curls espied :
The cheek a little pale, yet seeming so
As, if the lips could speak, the paleness soon would go.

* Vandyke's portrait of Waller's Sacharissa.

And rested there the lips, so warm and loving,
That, they *could* speak, one might be fain to guess :
Only they had been much too bright, if moving,
To stay by their own will, all motionless.
One outstretch'd hand its marble seal 'gan press
On roses which look'd fading ; while the eyes,
Uplifted in a calm, proud loveliness,
Seem'd busy with, their flow'ry destinies,
Drawing, for ladye's heart, some moral quaint and wise.

She perish'd like her roses. I did look
On her, as she did look on them—to sigh !
Alas, alas ! that the fair-written book
Of her sweet face, should be in death laid by,
As any blotted scroll ! Its cruelty
Poison'd a heart most gentle-pulsed of all,
And turn'd it unto song, therein to die :
For grief's stern tension maketh musical,
Unless the strain'd string break or ere the music fall.

Worship of Waller's heart ! no dream of thine
Reveal'd unto thee, that the lowly one,
Who sate enshadow'd near thy beauty's shine,
Should, when the light was out, the life was done,
Record thy name with those by Memory won
From Time's eternal burial. I am woo'd
By wholesome thoughts this sad thought hath begun,
For mind is strengthen'd when awhile subdued,
As he who touch'd the earth, and rose with power renew'd.

TO A POET'S CHILD.

A far harp swept the sea above;
A far voice said thy name in love:
Then silence on the harp was cast;
The voice was chain'd—the love went last!

And as I heard the melodie,
Sweet-voicëd Fancy spake of thee:
And as the silence o'er it came,
Mine heart, in silence, sigh'd thy name.

I thought there was one only place,
Where thou couldst lift thine orphan'd face
A little home for prayer and woe;—
A stone above—a shroud below;—

That evermore, that stone beside,
Thy wither'd joys would form thy pride;
As palm trees, on their south sea bed,
Make islands with the flowers they shed.

Child of the Dead! my dream of thee
Was sad to tell, and dark to see;
And vain as many a brighter dream;
Since thou canst sing by Babel's stream!

For here, amid the worldly crowd,
'Mid common brows, and laughter loud,
And hollow words, and feelings sere,
Child of the Dead! I meet thee here!

And is thy step so fast and light?
And is thy smile so gay and bright?
And *canst* thou smile, with cheek undim,
Upon a world that frown'd on *him*?

The minstrel's harp is on his bier ;
What doth the minstrel's orphan here ?
The loving moulders in the clay ;
The loved,—she keepeth holyday !

'Tis well ! I would not doom thy years
Of golden prime, to only tears.
Fair girl ! 'twere better that thine eyes
Should find a joy in summer skies,

As if their sun were on thy fate.
Be happy ; strive not to be great ;
And go not, from thy kind apart,
With lofty soul and stricken heart.

Think not too deeply : shallow thought,
Like open rills, is ever sought
By light and flowers ; while fountains deep
Amid the rocks and shadows sleep.

Feel not too warmly: lest thou be
Too like Cyrene's waters free,
Which burn at night, when all around
In darkness and in chill is found.

Touch not the harp to win the wreath:
Its tone is fame, its echo death!
The wreath may like the laurel grow,
Yet turns to cypress on the brow!

And, as a flame springs clear and bright,
Yet leaveth ashes 'stead of light;
So genius (fatal gift)! is doom'd
To leave the heart it fired, consumed.

For thee, for thee, thou orphan'd one,
I make an humble orison!
Love all the world; and ever dream
That all are true who truly seem.

Forget! for, so, 'twill move thee not,
Or lightly move; to be forgot!
Be streams thy music; hills, thy mirth;
Thy chiefest light, the household hearth.

So, when grief plays her natural part,
And visiteth thy quiet heart;
Shall all the clouds of grief be seen
To show a sky of hope between.

So, when thy beauty senseless lies,
No sculptured urn shall o'er thee rise;
But gentle eyes shall weep at will,
Such tears as hearts like thine distil.

MINSTRELSY.

One asked her once the resun why,
She hadde delyte in minstrelsie,
She answerëd on this manére.

Robert de Brunne.

For ever, since my childish looks
Could rest on Nature's pictured books;
For ever, since my childish tongue
Could name the themes our bards have sung;
So long, the sweetness of their singing
Hath been to me a rapture bringing!
Yet ask me not the reason why
I have delight in minstrelsy.

I know that much whereof I sing,
Is shapen but for vanishing ;
I know that summer's flower and leaf
And shine and shade are very brief,
And that the heart they brighten, may,
Before them all, be sheathed in clay !—
I do not know the reason why
I have delight in minstrelsy.

A few there are, whose smile and praise
My minstrel hope, would kindly raise :
But, of those few—Death may impress
The lips of some with silentness ;
While some may friendship's faith resign,
And heed no more a song of mine.—
Ask not, ask not the reason why
I have delight in minstrelsy.

The sweetest song that minstrels sing,
Will charm not Joy to tarrying;
The greenest bay that earth can grow,
Will shelter not in burning woe;
A thousand voices will not cheer,
When *one* is mute that aye is dear!—
Is there, alas! *no* reason why
I have delight in minstrelsy?

I do not know! The turf is green
Beneath the rain's fast-dropping sheen,
Yet asks not why that deeper hue
Doth all its tender leaves renew;—
And I, like-minded, am content,
While music to my soul is sent,
To question not the reason why
I have delight in minstrelsy.

Years pass—my life with them shall pass:
And soon, the cricket in the grass
And summer bird, shall louder sing
Than she who owns a minstrel's string.
Oh then may some, the dear and few,
Recall her love, whose truth they knew;
When all forget to question why
She had delight in minstrelsy!

TO THE MEMORY OF

SIR UVEDALE PRICE, BART.

FAREWELL !—a word that human lips bestow
On all that human hearts delight to know :
On summer skies, and scenes that change as fast ;
On ocean calms, and faith as fit to last ;
On Life, from Love's own arms, that breaks away ;
On hopes that blind, and glories that decay !

And ever thus, 'farewell, farewell,' is said,
As round the hills of lengthening time, we tread ;
As at each step, the winding ways unfold
Some untried prospect which obscures the old ;—

Perhaps a prospect brightly color'd o'er,
Yet not with brightness that we loved before ;
And dull and dark the brightest hue appears
To eyes like ours, surcharged and dim with tears.

Oft, oft we wish the winding road were past,
And yon supernal summit gain'd at last ;
Where all that gradual change removed, is found
At once, for ever, as you look around ;
Where every scene by tender eyes survey'd,
And lost and wept for, to their gaze is spread—
No tear to dim the sight, no shade to fall,
But Heaven's own sunshine lighting, charming all.

Farewell !—a common word—and yet how drear
And strange it soundeth as I write it here !
How strange that *thou* a place of death shouldst fill,
Thy brain unlighted, and thine heart grown chill !
And dark the eye, whose plausive glance to draw,
Incited Nature brake her tyrant's law !

And deaf the ear, to charm whose organ true,
Mœonian music tuned her harp anew !
And mute the lips where Plato's bee hath roved ;
And motionless the hand that genius moved !—
Ah friend ! thou speakest not !—but still to me
Do Genius, Music, Nature, speak of *thee !*—
Still golden fancy, still the sounding line,
And waving wood, recall some word of thine :
Some word, some look, whose living light is o'er—
And Memory sees what Hope can see no more.

Twice, twice, thy voice hath spoken. Twice there came
To us, a change, a joy—to thee, a fame !
Thou spakest once,* and every pleasant sight,
Woods waving wild, and fountains gushing bright,
Cool copses, grassy banks, and all the dyes
Of shade and sunshine gleam'd before our eyes.

* Essay on the Picturesque.

Thou spakest twice;* and every pleasant sound
Its ancient silken harmony unwound,
From Doric pipe and Attic lyre that lay
Enclasp'd in hands whose cunning is decay.
And now no more thou speakest! Death hath met
And won thee to him! Oh remember'd yet!
We cannot *see*, and *hearken*, and forget!

My thoughts are far. I think upon the time,
When Foxley's purple hills and woods sublime
Were thrilling at thy step; when thou didst throw
Thy burning spirit on the vale below,
To bathe its sense in beauty. Lovely ground!
There, never more shall step of thine resound!
There, Spring again shall come, but find thee not,
And deck with humid eyes her favorite spot;
Strew tender green on paths thy foot forsakes,
And make that fair, which Memory saddest makes.

* Essay on the Pronunciation of the Ancient Languages.

For me, all sorrowful, unused to raise
A minstrel song and dream not of thy praise,
Upon thy grave, my tuneless harp I lay,
Nor try to sing what only tears can say.
So warm and fast the ready waters swell—
So weak the faltering voice thou knewest well!
Thy words of kindness calm'd that voice before;
Now, thoughts of *them* but make it tremble more;
And leave its theme to others, and depart
To dwell within the silence where thou art.

THE AUTUMN.

Go, sit upon the lofty hill,
  And turn your eyes around,
Where waving woods and waters wild
  Do hymn an autumn sound.
The summer sun is faint on them—
  The summer flowers depart—
Sit still—as all transform'd to stone,
  Except your musing heart.

How there you sat in summer-time,
  May yet be in your mind;
And how you heard the green woods sing
  Beneath the freshening wind.

Though the same wind now blows around,
 You would its blast recall;
For every breath that stirs the trees,
 Doth cause a leaf to fall.

Oh! like that wind, is all the mirth
 That flesh and dust impart:
We cannot bear its visitings,
 When change is on the heart.
Gay words and jests may make us smile,
 When Sorrow is asleep;
But other things must make us smile,
 When Sorrow bids us *weep!*

The dearest hands that clasp our hands,—
 Their presence may be o'er;
The dearest voice that meets our ear,
 That tone may come no more!

Youth fades ; and then, the joys of youth,
Which once refresh'd our mind,
Shall come—as, on those sighing woods,
The chilling autumn wind.

Hear not the wind—view not the woods ;
Look out o'er vale and hill :
In spring, the sky encircled them—
The sky is round them still.
Come autumn's scathe—come winter's cold—
Come change—and human fate !
Whatever prospect HEAVEN doth bound,
Can ne'er be desolate.

THE DEATH-BED OF TERESA DEL RIEGO.

— Si fia muta ogni altra cosa, al fine
Parlerà il mio morire,
E ti dirà la morte il mio martire.

GUARINI.

The room was darken'd ; but a wan lamp shed
Its light upon a half-uncurtain'd bed,
Whereon the widow'd sate. Blackly as death
Her veiling hair hung round her, and no breath
Came from her lips to motion it. Between
Its parted clouds, the calm fair face was seen
In a snow paleness and snow silentness,
With eyes unquenchable, whereon did press
A little, their white lids, so taught to lie,
By weights of frequent tears wept secretly.

Her hands were clasp'd and raised—the lamp did fling
A glory on her brow's meek suffering.

Beautiful form of woman! seeming made
Alone to shine in mirrors, there to braid
The hair and zone the waist—to garland flowers—
To walk like sunshine through the orange bowers—
To strike her land's guitar—and often see
In other eyes how lovely hers must be.
Grew she acquaint with anguish? Did she sever
For ever from the one she loved for ever,
To dwell among the strangers? Ay! and she,
Who shone most brightly in that festive glee,
Sate down in this despair most patiently.

Some hearts are Niobes! In grief's down-sweeping,
They turn to very stone from over-weeping,
And after, feel no more. Hers did remain
In life, which is the power of feeling pain,

Till pain consumed the life so call'd below.
She heard that he was dead !—she ask'd not how—
For *he* was dead ! She wail'd not o'er his urn,
For *he* was dead—and in *her* hands, should burn
His vestal flame of honor radiantly,
Sighing would dim its light—she did not sigh.

She only died. They laid her in the ground,
Whereon th' unloving tread, and accents sound
Which are not of her Spain. She left behind,
For those among the strangers who were kind
Unto the poor heart-broken, her dark hair.
It once was gauded out with jewels rare;
It swept her dying pillow—it doth lie
Beside me, (thank the giver) droopingly,
And very long and bright ! Its tale doth go
Half to the dumb grave, half to life-time woe,
Making the heart of man, if manly, ring
Like Dodonæan brass, with echoing.

TO VICTOIRE, ON HER MARRIAGE.

VICTOIRE! I knew thee in thy land,
Where I was strange to all:
I heard thee; and were strange to me
The words thy lips let fall.

I loved thee—for the Babel curse
Was meant not for the heart:
I parted from thee, in such way
As those who love may part.

And now a change hath come to us,
A sea doth rush between!
I do not know if we can be
Again as we have been.

I sit down in mine English land,
  Mine English hearth beside;
And thou, to one I never knew,
  Art plighted for a bride.

It will not wrong thy present joy,
  With by-gone days to wend;
Nor wrongeth it mine English hearth,
  To love my Gallic friend.

Bind, bind the wreath! the slender ring
  Thy wedded fingers press!
May he who calls thy love his own,
  Call so thine happiness!

Be he Terpander to thine heart,
  And string fresh strings of gold,
Which may out-give new melodies,
  But never mar the old!

And though I clasp no more thy hand
  In my hand, and rejoice—
And though I see thy face no more,
  And hear no more thy voice—

Farewell, farewell!—let thought of me
  Visit thine heart! There is
In mine the very selfish prayer
  That prayeth for thy bliss!

TO A BOY.

WHEN my last song was said for thee,
Thy golden hair swept, long and free,
Around thee; and a dove-like tone
Was on thy voice—or Nature's own:
And every phrase and word of thine
Went out in lispings infantine!
Thy small steps faltering round our hearth—
Thine een out-peering in their mirth—
Blue een! that, like thine heart, seem'd given
To be, for ever, full of heaven!
Wert thou, in sooth, made up of glee,
When my last song was said for thee?

And now more years are finishëd,—
For thee another song is said.
Thy voice hath lost its cooing tone;
The lisping of thy words is gone:
Thy step treads firm—thine hair not flings
Round thee its length of golden rings—
Departed, like all lovely things!
Yet art thou still made up of glee,
When my *now* song is said for thee.

Wisely and well responded they,
Who cut thy golden hair away,
What time I made the bootless prayer,
That they should pause awhile, and spare.
They said, 'its sheen did less agree
With boyhood than with infancy.'
And thus I know it aye must be.
Before the revel noise is done,
The revel lamps pale one by one.

Ay! Nature loveth not to bring
Crown'd victims to life's labouring.
The mirth-effulgent eye appears
Less sparkling—to make room for tears:
After the heart's quick throbs depart,
We lose the gladness of the heart:
And, after we have lost awhile
The rose o' the lip, we lose its smile;
As Beauty could not bear to press
Near the death-pyre of Happiness.

This seemeth but a sombre dream?
It hath more pleasant thoughts than seem.
The older a young tree doth grow,
The deeper shade it sheds below;
But makes the grass more green—the air
More fresh, than had the sun been there.
And thus our human life is found,
Albeit a darkness gather round:

For patient virtues, that their light
May shine to all men, want the night :
And holy Peace, unused to cope,
Sits meekly at the tomb of Hope,
Saying that 'she is risen!'
Then I
Will sorrow not at destiny,—
Though from thine eyes, and from thine heart,
The glory of their light depart ;
Though on thy voice, and on thy brow,
Should come a fiercer change than now ;
Though thou no more be made of glee,
When my next song is said for thee.

REMONSTRANCE.

Oh say not it is vain to weep
   That deafen'd bier above;
Where genius has made room for death,
   And life is past from love;
That tears can never his bright looks
   And tender words restore:
I know it is most vain to weep—
   And therefore, weep the more!

Oh say not I shall cease to weep
   When years have wither'd by;
That ever I shall speak of joy,
   As if he could reply;

That ever mine unquivering lips
  Shall name the name he bore:
I know that I may cease to weep,
  And therefore weep the more!

Say, Time, who slew mine happiness,
  Will leave to me my woe;
And woe's own stony strength shall chain
  These tears' impassion'd flow:
Or say, that these, my ceaseless tears,
  May life to death restore;
For then my soul were wept away,
  And I should weep no more!

Reply.

To weep awhile beside the bier,
  Whereon his ashes lie,
Is well!—I know that rains must fall
  When clouds are in the sky:

I know, *to die—to part*, will cloud
  The brightest spirit o'er;
And yet, wouldst *thou* for ever weep,
  When *he* can weep no more?

Fix not thy sight, so long and fast,
  Upon the shroud's despair;
Look upward unto Zion's hill,
  For death was also *there*!
And think, 'The death, the scourge, the scorn,
  My sinless Saviour bore—
The curse—the pang, too deep for tears—
  That *I* should weep no more!'

EPITAPH.

BEAUTY, who softly walkest all thy days,
In silken garment to the tunes of praise ;—
Lover, whose dreamings by the green-bank'd river,
Where once she wander'd, fain would last for ever ;—
King, whom the nations scan, adoring scan,
And shout 'a god,' when sin hath mark'd thee man ;—
Bard, on whose brow the Hyblan dew remains,
Albeit the fever burneth in the veins ;—
Hero, whose sword in tyrant's blood is hot ;—
Sceptic, who doubting, wouldst be doubted not ;—
Man, whosoe'er thou art, whate'er thy trust ;—
Respect thyself in me ;—thou treadest *dust.*

THE IMAGE OF GOD.

"I am God, and there is none like me.'

ISAIAH xlvi. 9.

"Christ, who is the image of God.'

2 COR. iv. 4.

Thou ! art thou like to God ?
(I ask'd this question of the glorious sun)
Thou high unwearied one,
Whose course in heat, and light, and life is run ?

Eagles may view thy face—clouds can assuage
Thy fiery wrath—the sage
Can mete thy stature —thou shalt fade with age,
Thou art not like to God.

Thou! art thou like to God?
(I ask'd this question of the bounteous earth)
Oh thou, who givest birth
To forms of beauty and to sounds of mirth?

In all thy glory works the worm decay—
Thy golden harvests stay
For seed and toil—thy power shall pass away.
Thou art not like to God.

Thou! art thou like to God?
(I ask'd this question of my deathless soul)
Oh thou, whose musings roll
Above the thunder, o'er creation's whole?

Thou art not. Sin, and shame, and agony
Within thy deepness lie:
They utter forth their voice in thee, and cry
'*Thou* art not like to God.'

Then art THOU like to God ;
Thou, who didst bear the sin, and shame, and woe—
O Thou, whose sweat did flow—
Whose tears did gush— whose brow was dead and low ?

No grief is like thy grief ; no heart can prove
Love like unto thy love ;
And none, save only Thou,—below, above,—
Oh God, is like to God !

THE APPEAL.

CHILDREN of our England! stand
On the shores that girt our land;
The ægis of whose cloud-white rock
Braveth Time's own battle shock.
Look above the wide, wide world;
Where the northern blasts have furl'd
Their numbëd wings amid the snows,
Mutt'ring in a forced repose—
Or where the madden'd sun on high
Shakes his torch athwart the sky,
Till within their prison sere,
Chainëd earthquakes groan for fear?

Look above the wide, wide world,
Where a gauntlet Sin hath hurl'd
To astonied Life ; and where
Death's gladiatorial smile doth glare,
On making the arena bare.
Shout aloud the words that show
Jesus in the sands and snow ;—
Shout aloud the words that free,
Over the perpetual sea.

Speak ye. As a breath will sweep
Avalanche from Alpine steep,
So the spoken word shall roll
Fear and darkness from the soul.
Are ye men, and love not man ?
Love ye, and permit his ban ?
Can ye, dare ye, rend the chain
Wrought of common joy and pain,

Clasping with its links of gold,
Man to man in one strong hold?
Lo! if the golden links ye sever,
Ye shall make your heart's flesh quiver;
And wheresoe'er the links are reft,
There, shall be a blood-stain left.
To earth's remotest rock repair,
Ye shall find a vulture there:
Though for others sorrowing not,
Your own tears shall still be hot:
Though ye play a lonely part;
Though ye bear an iron heart;—
Woe, like Echetus, still must
Grind your iron into dust.

But children of our Britain, ye
Rend not man's chain of sympathy;
To those who sit in woe and night,
Denying tears and hiding light.

Ye have stretch'd your hands abroad
With the Spirit's sheathless sword :
Ye have spoken—and the tone
To earth's extremest verge hath gone :
East and west sublime it rolls,
Echoed by a million souls !
The wheels of rapid circling years,
Erst hot with crime, are quench'd in tears.
Rocky hearts wild waters pour,
That were chain'd in stone before :
Bloody hands, that only bare
Hilted sword, are clasp'd in prayer :
Savage tongues, that wont to fling
Shout of war in deathly ring,
Speak the name which angels sing.
Dying lips are lit the while
With a most undying smile,
Which reposing there, instead
Of language, when the lips are dead,

Saith,—'No sound of grief or pain,
Shall haunt us when we move again.'

Children of our country! brothers
To the children of all others!
Shout aloud the words that show
Jesus in the sands and snow;—
Shout aloud the words that free,
Over the perpetual sea!

IDOLS.

How weak the gods of this world are--
  And weaker yet their worship made me!
I have been an idolater
  Of three—and three times they betray'd me.

Mine oldest worshipping was given
  To natural Beauty, aye residing
In bowery earth and starry heav'n,
  In ebbing sea, and river gliding.

But natural Beauty shuts her bosom
  To what the natural feelings tell!
Albeit I sigh'd, the trees would blossom—
  Albeit I smiled, the blossoms fell.

Then left I earthly sights, to wander
  Amid a grove of name divine,
Where bay-reflecting streams meander,
  And Moloch Fame hath rear'd a shrine.

Not green, but black, is that reflection ;
  On rocky beds those waters lie ;
That grove hath chilness and dejection—
  How could I sing? I had to sigh.

Last, human Love, thy Lares greeting,
  To rest and warmth I vow'd my years.
To rest? how wild my pulse is beating!
  To warmth? ah me! my burning tears.

Ay! *they* may burn—though thou be frozen
  By death, and changes wint'ring on!
Fame—Beauty!—idols madly chosen—
  Were yet of gold; but *thou* art STONE!

Crumble like stone! my voice no longer
  Shall wail their names, who silent be:
There is a voice that soundeth stronger—
  'My daughter, give thine heart to *me*.'

Lord! take mine heart! Oh first and fairest,
  Whom all creation's ends shall hear;
Who deathless love in death declarest!
  None else is beauteous—famous—dear!

HYMN.

"Lord, I cry unto thee, make haste unto me."
PSALM cxli.

"The Lord is nigh unto them that call upon him.
PSALM cxlv.

SINCE without Thee we do no good,
  And with Thee do no ill,
Abide with us in weal and woe,—
  In action and in will.

In weal,—that while our lips confess
  The Lord who 'gives,' we may
Remember, with an humble thought,
  The Lord who 'takes away.'

In woe,—that, while to drowning tears
  Our hearts their joys resign,
We may remember *who* can turn
  Such water into wine.

By hours of day,—that when our feet
  O'er hill and valley run,
We still may think the light of truth
  More welcome than the sun.

By hours of night,—that when the air
  Its dew and shadow yields,
We still may hear the voice of God
  In silence of the fields.

Oh! then sleep comes on us like death,
  All soundless, deaf and deep:
Lord! teach us so to watch and pray,
  That death may come like sleep.

Abide with *us*, abide with *us*,
  While flesh and soul agree;
And when our flesh is only dust,
  Abide our souls with *Thee*.

WEARINESS.

MINE eyes are weary of surveying
The fairest things, too soon decaying;
Mine ears are weary of receiving
The kindest words—ah, past believing!
Weary my hope, of ebb and flow;
Weary my pulse, of tunes of woe:
My trusting heart is weariest!
I would—I would, I were at rest!

For *me*, can earth refuse to fade?
For *me*, can words be faithful made?
Will *my* embitter'd hope be sweet?
My pulse forego the human beat?

No ! Darkness must consume mine eye—
Silence, mine ear—hope cease—pulse die—
And o'er mine heart a stone be press'd—
Or vain this,—' Would I were at rest !'

There is a land of rest deferr'd :
Nor eye hath seen, nor ear hath heard,
Nor Hope hath trod the precinct o'er ;
For hope beheld is hope no more !
There, human pulse forgets its tone—
There, hearts may know as they are known !
Oh, for dove's wings, thou dwelling blest,
To fly to *thee*, and be at rest !

THE END.

www.ingramcontent.com/pod-product-compliance
Lightning Source LLC
LaVergne TN
LVHW010245110826
845151LV00004B/1400
9781425523268